Child Language
and Cognition

Child Language Acquisition Series— Titles in Preparation

Marion Blank, Ph.D., et al. *Developmental Discourse Therapy: Using Basic Research for Effective Intervention*

Stan A. Kuczaj II, Ph.D. *Children's Acquisition of Word Meanings*

Carol Stoel-Gammon, Ph.D., and Carla Dunn, Ph. D. *Normal and Disordered Phonology in Children*

Helen Tager-Flusberg, Ph.D. *The Acquisition of Syntax*

Ina Č. Užgiris, Ph.D. *Communication: The Foundation for Language*

A University Park Press
Topicbook

The University Park Press Topicbooks are carefully selected, written, and designed to identify the issues and controversies in communication science and disorders, to help readers find their way through the broad range of information available, and to serve as short topical introductions for professionals and students.

Child Language and Cognition

Contemporary Issues

Mabel L. Rice, Ph.D.

Associate Professor, Department of Speech-Language-Hearing; Child Language Graduate Program, The University of Kansas–Lawrence

Susan Kemper, Ph.D.

Associate Professor, Department of Psychology; Child Language Graduate Program, The University of Kansas–Lawrence

University Park Press • Baltimore

University Park Press
International Publishers in Medicine and Allied Health
300 North Charles Street
Baltimore, Maryland 21201

Sponsoring editor: Janet S. Hankin
Production editor: Megan Barnard Shelton
Cover design by: Caliber Design Planning, Inc.
Series logo by: Barry Goldman Designs
Typeset by: Waldman Graphics, Inc.
Manufactured in the United States of America by: Halliday Lithograph

Library of Congress Cataloging in Publication Data
Rice, Mabel.
    Child language and cognition.
    (Child language acquisition series) (A University Park
Press topicbook)
    Bibliography: p. 125
    Includes index.
    1. Language acquisition.   2. Cognition.   3. Communica-
tive competence.   I. Kemper, Susan.   II. Title.
III. Series.
P118.R49   1984   401'.9   84-7492
ISBN 0-8391-1870-8

Contents

Preface to the *Child Language Acquisition* Series

The study of child language acquisition has emerged, in the past 15 years, as a distinct and rapidly growing field of inquiry, located at the intersection of several established disciplines. The books included in the *Child Language Acquisition* series cover key topics in this growing and diverse literature. The goal of each volume is to summarize the research knowledge of a particular aspect of language acquisition, synthesizing different theoretical perspectives and academic disciplines. Within each volume the range of children's achievement of language acquisition is addressed, from the apparently effortless mastery by normally developing children to the limited or unusual language acquired by atypical children.

The books are written for advanced undergraduate and graduate students as well as for professionals providing service to children and researchers in related disciplines. Each volume is written at an introductory level, with clear definitions of terms, substantive discussions of major theoretical and empirical issues, and judicious referencing of original sources. The topics will include the sources of language (biological, cognitive, social, and environmental), aspects of language (phonology, word meaning, grammar, and discourse), and patterns of atypical acquisition (developmental language disorders, learning disabilities, mental retardation, deafness, and bilingualism). The books can be grouped or used individually in courses covering such topics as child language acquisition, cognitive development, social development, and education of young children.

Child Language and Cognition: Contemporary Issues, by Rice and Kemper, provides a fresh and readable account of contemporary research on one of the most fundamental questions in the study of child development: the relationship of language and cognition. Research on this topic has both theoretical and applied significance, in that it may illuminate the development of linguistic and nonlinguistic cognition, as well as suggest innovative intervention and assessment procedures for children with handicapping conditions. Drawing on a remarkable range of research in fields as disparate as linguistic theory, anthropology, sociolinguistics, cognitive theory and development, speech pathology, and education, the authors have illustrated the many possible connections of language and cognition, and the plausibility of each in particular contexts. As they point out, the "mapping problem" does not have a single solution. An adequate representation of the relationship between language and cognition must take into account the multifaceted nature of both language and cognition: the many kinds of linguistic and nonlinguistic knowledge constructed by children.

Preface

Many have written about the relationships between what children know and how they learn to talk. It is our purpose to summarize, comment upon, and synthesize what has become a formidably large and technical literature. We have attempted to do this at a level intermediate between an introductory textbook and a scholarly research monograph. Our intended audience is the wide array of professional colleagues and graduate students who have an interest in the issues involved in the intersection of children's thinking and talking.

The basic questions are causal in nature: for example, does cognition account for early language acquisition, or does language shape thought? Such causal questions must be answered with respect to the full range of children's development. We believe that the study of disordered or minimal development can illuminate the factors or processes that account for normal or accelerated development. The possible circumstances can be illustrated in a matrix:

		Language Acquisition	
		Normal	*Disordered*
Cognitive Development	*Normal*	A	B
	Deficient	C	D

Traditional theories of children's language and cognition have focused on the children of Cell A. On the other hand, there is a new and growing literature describing the children who fall into Cells B, C, and D. The contemporary commitment to educational programming for handicapped children has led to recent studies of children who are deaf or have language disorders (Cell B), or who are mentally retarded with normal (Cell C) or deficient language (Cell D). Observations of the skills of the children in Cells B, C, and D challenge the assumptions of traditional accounts of the cognition-language relationship.

Our purview of the available literature is broad, although it is restricted to recent work (most of our primary sources were published within the last 15 years). The result is a horizontal survey of academic disciplines, scholarly paradigms, and the developmental levels ranging from infancy to adolescence. Pertinent writings are drawn from developmental psychology, social psychology, cognitive psychology, linguistics, philosophy, speech and language disorders, and education. Concepts and issues are conveyed in a common terminology, with appropriate definitions and illustrations.

This range of research and theory reflects the joint expertise of the authors. Rice brings a background of speech pathology and developmental psychology. Kemper is a psycholinguist. They share a strong interest in child language.

Our intended audience spans the range of the contributing disciplines. We have written for our professional colleagues who want to know about the contemporary literature but who do not have time available to digest diverse and paradigm-specific writings; they include academic scholars and educational practitioners. The volume could serve well as a primary source book for a graduate seminar in child language or cognitive development. It could also be used as supplemental reading for undergraduate and graduate classes in child development, language disorders, or special education in the areas of learning disabilities, education of the deaf, and mental retardation.

The first chapter provides an orientation to the central issues in the contemporary debates about the relationship between children's thought and language acquisition. Key terms in theories of language and cognition are defined and illustrated. The second and third chapters describe competing theoretical models. These models address the earliest stages of language acquisition. The initial inspiration was the striking parallel between toddlers' first linguistic meanings and Piaget's account of young children's earliest concepts. Initial Piagetian interpretations of language acquisition led to counterproposals and subsequent revision of early models.

The fourth chapter presents notions that have been overshadowed by the dominant debates about children's mastery of object terms. The conceptual framework associated with language is not limited to object knowledge. Knowledge of persons, social categories, and event sequences are essential for children's full use and understanding of language.

In Chapters 5 and 6 the focus shifts beyond the early stages of language to the child's mastery of formal grammar and the use of language as a cognitive tool. The relationship between emerging logical thought and syntactic structures is discussed in Chapter 5. In Chapter 6, the child is assumed to be a competent user of language, and the implications of language as a possible facilitator, adjunct, or inhibitor of mental processes are considered.

The final chapter serves a number of related goals. Retrospectively, we summarize the major points of the preceding chapters and provide our conclusions. Prospectively, we project some future lines of work. Finally, we describe our own synthesis, a model of children's linguistic and cognitive growth. We have adopted a metaphor from the area of horticulture; it is one familiar to developmentalists yet not previously applied to the cognition/language issue. We believe it captures the complexity of the interrelationships more adequately than do more simplistic models.

We would like to thank those who helped in the development of the book. Janet S. Hankin, senior editor at University Park Press, has been supportive and encouraging throughout. Several colleagues read earlier drafts and provided helpful comments: Jon Bonvillian, Philip Dale, Catherine Snow, Ina Uzgiris, and several anonymous reviewers. Detailed feedback was provided by graduate students Thurma DeLoach, Sharon Linville, and Barbara Zaremski. Preparation of the manuscript was accomplished with the help of Carrie Freesman, Patsy Horner, Michael Hughes, and Lisa Jerry.

Parts of Chapter 2 appeared in an article by Rice published in the *Journal of Speech and Hearing Disorders* (1983). Much of Chapter 3 is part of a longer chapter by Rice that appears in Schiefelbusch and Pickar's *The Acquisition of Communicative Competence* (1984), a volume in the *Language Intervention Series* published by University Park Press.

Support for manuscript preparation was provided by a grant from the Spencer Foundation to the Center for Research on the Influence of Television on Children.

Chapter 1

The Mapping Problem—Basic Distinctions and Definitions

The acquisition of language is a commonplace miracle. Children all over the world, in markedly differing circumstances, learn to talk. They have something to say and the means to express their thoughts. Even before children begin to talk, their first primitive communication is about things in their world. They tug on their parents' clothes to attract full attention as they point and grunt to indicate the object of their desire. Children's first words are typically about objects. They comment on the existence of things, the disappearance or reoccurrence of objects, the location and ownership and actions of objects. These early linguistic meanings are evident in different languages and different cultures. When children learn to talk, they talk about what they know, and what they know centers around the things in their world.

This fascination with objects is consistent with a well-known theory of the knowledge structures of young children that was proposed by Jean Piaget. According to his account, toddlers first work out a set of meanings or understandings based on their interactions with objects and search for a means of expressing these meanings. The match between meanings and words serves as a key for the mastery of language.

This is a deceptive characterization of children's early language acquisition. It first appeared in the contemporary child language literature in the early 1970s and scholars have discussed, debated, and investigated it since. Controversy arose over the direction of influence and the relative contribution of meanings compared to other factors. As competing accounts appeared, the fundamental nature of the basic issues—the underlying epistemological context—became apparent. Interwoven in the arguments are such issues as: the nature of cognition and language and the amount of overlap between them, the direction and strength of influence; developmental universals; innate versus environmental influences; and commonalities across children versus individual differences. Given such timeless issues, the modern controversies are extensions of traditional lines of argument that have deep historical roots. The contemporary debate has led to an avalanche of empirical evidence and to methodological critiques of the ways in which such evidence is collected and interpreted.

The modern cognition/language question is particularly relevant because of its educational implications. Traditional concern has focused on the enhancement of the progress of normally developing children, as a reflection of society's commitment to educate those children. However, concurrent with the rapid expansion of the child language literature, the educational franchise has expanded to include handicapped children, including infants. The social commitment to educate handicapped children has supported empirical research to explore the nature of their problems, as well as to design and provide appropriate remediation.

The question of the relationship between cognition and language is especially important in the case of children with difficulties acquiring language. Contrary to the assumption that all children learn language in an effortless manner, some children struggle unsuccessfully to do so. A conservative estimate is that 1 out of 100 children in the United States under age 5 experiences difficulty in language acquisition; the estimate rises to 2 out of 100 for children ages 5 to 14 (Fein, 1983). Some of those children have associated problems that contribute to the language difficulties, such as mental retardation or hearing impairment. The majority of them, however, are children whose only, or major, problem is that of language acquisition. These children have normal intelligence, normal perceptual and neuromotor abilities, and age-appropriate social and emotional responses, yet their language skills are below age expectations. The usual term for this group, and the one that is used here, is "language-disordered children." It is perplexing that their developmental problems are limited to language. Recent investigations have pursued the question of whether or not more general cognitive problems are implicated in the difficulty with verbal symbols.

Children with language problems present special educational

difficulties. They often have related academic deficits—reading in particular is troublesome. Many are identified as learning disabled. For children with additional handicaps, such as a physical disability or mental retardation, it is often difficult to ascertain the extent of the problems due to language or to determine if language abilities are constrained by other limitations. Educators daily confront the question "Does he not know, or does he not have the means to tell me what he knows?"

The contemporary concern with atypical as well as normal children creates new sources of evidence and new applications of the literature. Historically, observations of children in unusual developmental circumstances, such as deaf, mute, or neurologically impaired children, have served as supporting evidence for theoretical formulations regarding the nature of human mental capacities. In similar fashion, recent writings regarding the role of cognition in language acquisition are buttressed by new findings with handicapped children. The emergence of scholars whose primary concern is remediation brings a modern critical perspective, an assessment of explanations vis-à-vis their extension to the educational management of language-disordered children. The applied perspective can serve as a rigorous screening, separating the robust aspects of the normative literature from the speculative, and revealing the gaps in current knowledge.

The content of this book is an overview of the current literature addressing the relationship between children's linguistic and nonlinguistic knowledge, especially at the early stages of language acquisition. Our frame of reference is that of children's development, not the nature of human knowledge, phylogenetic origins of language, or species-specific linguistic competence. Those basic issues have inspired much of the germinal work in the area, and constitute its most general context. Our intent is to capture the gist of contemporary writings, to identify key issues and themes, to selectively review relevant literature, and to summarize current conclusions. As a result we point out existing gaps in knowledge and identify emerging issues.

Preliminary Distinctions and Definitions

The language/congition debate invites a rather casual use of terms and a blurring of conceptual distinctions. The literature is characterized by an inconsistent use of key expressions and a shifting set of basic assumptions. Given this state of affairs, some preliminary distinctions and definitions are in order. They serve as reference points for the subsequent discussion and as indicators of our perspective on certain matters.

The Main Issue: The Mapping Problem

Eve Clark (1973a, 1975, 1977) introduced the phrase "mapping problems" to describe the heart of the issue. It involves the assumption that there are two different kinds of knowing, nonlinguistic and linguistic, that are not isomorphic with each other. The child's problem is to accomplish a match between the two, to map one onto the other. For adults the matching is so automatic and apparently complete that the distinction and the problem are not intuitively obvious. However, the two kinds of knowledge never fully correspond even for adults.

The situation is depicted in Figure 1. Nonlinguistic knowledge is on the bottom because it is more basic (it appears first ontogenetically and is less vulnerable to cerebral malfunction or fatigue effects). Linguistic knowledge is above the nonlinguistic base (as a higher-order kind of knowing) and offset, to indicate the lack of 1:1 correspondence between the two. The proportion of the overlap changes ontogenetically: there is no overlap for the prelinguistic infant, who knows a little about the world but nothing about language. With language acquisition, the amount of

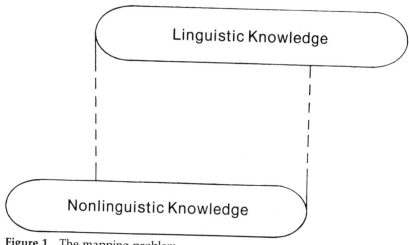

Figure 1 The mapping problem.

overlap increases to some stable and mature, yet incomplete, proportion.

The part of nonlinguistic knowledge that extends to the left in Figure 1 represents the aspects of knowing that are resistant to linguistic expression and remain largely outside it. Examples are physical skills, such as riding a bike or typing, and knowledge of spatial relationships. It is very difficult to tell someone how to ride a bike; the location of a particular key on the typewriter is more accessible by reenactment of typing motions than verbal description; giving directions is easier with a map than words.

The part of linguistic knowledge that extends to the right in Figure 1 represents the kinds of linguistic knowledge that are not tied to underlying meanings. An example is provided by McCawley (1971), who observed that, although speakers of English can say *put on the hat* or *put it on*, they cannot say *put on it*. Such constraints are of a formal, grammatical nature, beyond the meanings expressed. Other examples include such arbitrary dialectal differences as a preference for *stand in line* among one group of English speakers contrasted with *stand on line* for others, or *graduate high school* for some, compared to *graduate from high school* for others. The influence of grammatical structures on the expression of meaning has recently been recognized by those linguists who originally argued for a strong role for meanings in accounting for formal structures (Fillmore, 1977). For example, the choice of a verb constrains the syntactic roles of the noun arguments associated with the verb. Bowerman (1982a, p. 182) provided illustrations using the contrastive pairs *sold/bought* and *pour/fill*. We can say *Harry sold a car to John* and *John bought a car from Harry*, but not *John sold a car from Harry* or *Harry bought a car to John*. We can say *John poured water into a cup* and *John filled the cup with water*, but not *John poured the cup with water* or *John filled water into the cup*.

The fact that these examples involve language-specific knowledge of a rather formal sort may be most apparent from a child's perspective. Such arbitrary constraints prove troublesome for children, even those who seem to have all the underlying meanings worked out, as is evident in the kinds of errors they make (illustrated in Bowerman, 1982a). There is reason to suspect that such arbitrary aspects of language may be especially difficult for language-disordered children, although there is little evidence pertinent to the point. The reliance on models of grammar based on underlying meanings has deflected investigators' attention from this possibility.

Given that cognition and language each have their own domains, there is also a sizeable area of overlap. Linkages between meanings and language are possible, as indicated by the dotted lines in Figure 1. Such linkages are not automatically accomplished, nor is the correspondence between linguistic and cognitive categories inherently obvious. Nonlinguistic categories do not directly map onto particular linguistic forms; some adjustments are necessary in order to accomplish a fit. This is most evident in cross-linguistic comparisons. Languages vary in regard to which meanings are encoded in language and the means by which they are coded. Although children's cognitive knowledge base may be universally similar in content and organization, their commonly and individually held concepts must be adjusted to correspond to their native language. Slobin (1979) demonstrated the mapping problem by recasting the English sentence *Daddy gave me the ball* into its equivalent representation in German, Hebrew, and Turkish. He notes that the four languages differ in regard to the meanings represented (e.g., definite versus indefinite objects, sex of actors, time of action, direct versus indirect experience) and how these distinctions are coded in language (word order, morphemes, lexical items). Schlesinger (1977, p. 156) pointed out that such grammatically relevant categories as "agent" are not independent of language. Children must work out what constitutes an agent (Mommy handing the bottle to the child? Mommy just holding the bottle?) for the particular language to be learned. Languages thus differ in the nonlinguistic meanings that are bundled together into various grammatical contrasts. Such rebundling is also evident at the level of words, where cross-linguistic differences are numerous. A few examples: in English, we *open* screw-top containers and boxes, among other things, but not light switches and electrical appliances, although the corresponding word in other languages does apply to those contexts. In English, we *put on* our hats, shoes, dresses, trousers, shirts, gloves and rings, but, in Japanese, speakers learn different words for different actions on different parts of the body.

Educators and speech clinicians are prone to overlook the mapping problem encountered by children, especially in the area of word meanings. Many traditional pedagogical procedures are based on the assumption that the child who has a nonlinguistic notion, such as a set of cuplike objects, has only the task of associating a label with that notion. We tend to overlook the fact that the perceptual and functional similarities that may initially determine the nonlinguistic category do not always correspond to the boundaries of the linguistic category. A common styrofoam container for hot drinks is called *cup* but actually looks like a *glass*. An intervening step is necessary to rework the nonlinguistic notion to conform with the arbitrary boundaries of the linguistic category. An awareness of this reworking process, the mapping problem, could be applied to an analysis of the nature of children's error in training, and thereby help us to focus our training efforts on the process itself where necessary.

Definitions of Cognition and Language

The preceding discussion of the mapping problem simplified the explanation by treating "nonlinguistic knowledge" and "linguistic knowledge" as single units. Of course, they really are not simple homogenous clumps; instead each is complex and multifaceted, with rather complicated interactions. Unfortunately, a definitive, comprehensive model, representing widespread scholarly acceptance, does not presently exist for either language or cognition. However, some general distinctions have achieved conventional status. We sketch out those that have been prominent in the literature, with two purposes in mind: to identify key notions and terms, and to specify the intended meanings of terms that often have vague or overlapping senses.

Cognition

In this discussion, "cognition" refers to knowledge of a nonlinguistic nature. Although language learning is usually regarded as a cognitive task, and rightfully so, the term "cognition" here is used in a more specific sense to contrast it with the domain of language. Two levels of cognition relevant to language acquisition have been differentiated (Bowerman, 1978b; Cromer, 1976): a superficial level of thoughts, intentions, and meanings, and a deeper level of cognitive structures. Among the cognitive units of the superficial level are categories and concepts, two terms often used synonymously. The notion of "category" has a formal operational definition that is the basis of many experimental studies. Evidence of a category (concept) is generally defined as the same observable response (action or word label) for a series of discriminably different events (stimuli). Classically, a category is regarded as resulting from an underlying, dynamic rule-governed mental process (Bruner, Goodnow, & Austin, 1956). Much of the confusion between concept and word may be a consequence of traditional psychological experimentation in which word labels served as evidence and/or definitions of categories, e.g., *red/color, circle/shape,* or *three/ number.*

The notion of categories dominates debates over the role of cognition in children's language acquisition, especially in regard to the mapping problem. In order to master the adult mapping of language and cognition, children must possess the appropriate nonlinguistic categories and the correct rules for establishing categorical equivalences. Generally, the term "category" has a broad range of application, meant to imply any set of equivalent things, where "things" refers to not only objects, but also actions, events, and their attributes; the attributes of objects, actions, and events include the obvious ones of parts and physical characteristics, such as color and shape, as well as functional capabilities and relationships, such as taller than or longer than (e.g., Mervis & Rosch, 1981, p. 108). Categorical equivalences are not limited to objects, actions, and events; individuals and social relationships may be categorized by relative status and social stereotypes (e.g., Cantor & Mischel, 1979). Things are categorized by the application of equivalence rules such as possession of a criterial feature, resemblance to a category prototype, or specifications by examples. Different categories may arise from different rule-governed processes.

The term "concept" has a less formal connotation. It is used as a synonym for category as well as to refer to general ideas or notions. Concept often means roughly the same as "a unit of meaning underlying language." Some writers (e.g., Slobin, 1973) have used intentions and others (e.g., Karmiloff-Smith, 1979) have used functions in much the same sense, in contrast to the common use of intentions and functions to refer to the pragmatic aspects of language (requests, comments, denials, etc.). In this discussion, concept refers to ideas, thoughts, understandings, or meanings that may or may not conform to categorical structure.

The deeper level of cognitive understanding associated with studies of language acquisition is that of mental structure, a term describing abstract organizational patterns that control cognitive functioning. According to Piaget, children derive their own mental structures from their interactions with their environment. The basic structures are common to all children and evolve in the same sequence of stages. More recently, the term "mental schemata" has been used to describe other sorts of cognitive structures for spatially, causally, and temporally ordered information. For example, young children know the usual location of objects in rooms and the usual order of events in a familiar sequence. Such knowledge is described as schematic in nature. The notion of schema is emerging as a general explanatory construct, with some theorists arguing that young children's knowledge is organized schematically rather than categorically (Mandler, 1983). Temporally and causally organized understanding is referred to as event knowledge, evident in children's ability to relate familiar sequences, such as the steps involved in baking cookies, and to behave in a manner appropriate for expected sequences, such as knowing what will happen next when dining in a restaurant. The notion of event knowledge has relevance for certain aspects of children's linguistic knowledge.

The notion of structure has influenced child language researchers in several ways. First, it provides deep-seated, abstract cognitive knowledge that is directly analogous to Chomsky's notion of deep linguistic structures; such deeply rooted understanding is regarded as the unseen framework interrelating many superficially different bits of knowledge. Second, mental structures are quite consistent with the contemporary conclusion that children's linguistic performance is rule governed. This parallel has been pursued in a number of studies comparing syntax or formal linguistic structures with cognitive structures.

A particularly useful aspect of Piagetian structures is their content. Such Piagetian notions as object permanence and conservation correspond to what children talk about, the meanings that are available for language. These constructs lead to predictions about links between different structures and the particulars of linguistic acquisition. Finally, Piaget's claim that cognitive structures are rooted in infants' actions upon objects has been particularly salient for child language scholars interested in the earliest stages of language acquisition.

Closely related to the idea of cognitive structure is that of cognitive operation, another term rooted in Piaget's theory. Structures are formations of operations. Operations "concern transformations of reality by means of internalized actions that are grouped into coherent, reversible systems" (Piaget & Inhelder, 1969, p. 93). An example of a Piagetian operation that has been associated with language is reversibility, which involves knowing that for any particular mental action its opposite can be applied, thereby returning to the initial state (e.g., adding two things to one thing makes three things, and subtracting two things from three things leaves the original one thing; pouring water from a short, wide container into a tall, thin container does not change the amount, because the action can be reversed). This cognitive rule has been compared with children's ability to order elements of sentences and their use of comparative terms, such as *more* and *less*, or *taller* and *tallest*.

A notion central to Piaget's account of language acquisition is that of mental representation. It is the ability to recall or represent to oneself objects or events not immediately present (see Mandler, 1983, for a more detailed delineation of the different senses of the term, and how Piaget used it). Obviously, the use of language depends on the ability to represent the not-here and not-now with words. Piaget argued that evidence of mental representation was apparent in prelinguistic toddlers in their capacity for symbolic play, deferred imitation, and recognition of pictured objects and in their sense of permanence of objects. Two of these, symbolic play and object permanence, have been prominently linked with emerging linguistic knowledge. Symbolic play involves pretending that one object is another, or pretending actions associated with other circumstances. Children who use a pencil as a telephone receiver are regarded as able mentally to picture the telephone receiver while knowing the pencil has other uses; children who pretend to sleep when it is not bedtime, in a play situation, know that the behavior is appropriate for another time and place. Object permanence refers to children's knowledge that objects do not disappear when they are out of sight. Instead, they can imagine objects to be where they are even when concealed. Such awareness is evident in the search strategies and behaviors of toddlers, who will tug on a covering cloth to reveal a hidden object, or look for a toy train to emerge from the end of the tunnel opposite the one it entered.

Piaget did not address such basic psychological processes as memory, attention, auditory sequencing, patterning and recall, hierarchical planning, detection and recognition of individual cues, properties or features as well as patterns of information, and so on. These mental processes are involved in the transfer of cognitive knowledge to linguistic understanding. Although scholars readily acknowledge their importance, during the 1970s these processes have been overshadowed by the explanatory promise of Piaget's more abstract and encompassing notions.

Another consequence of the dominance of Piaget's account of early development is a tendency to limit considerations of young children's cognitive knowledge to that which is object based, a tendency that is consistent with traditional experimental paradigms. However, as pointed out earlier in regard to categories, not all of children's understandings are based in objects. Early on they are aware of social categories, such as the roles people assume (e.g., mother, teacher), and of person-based attributes, such as states (e.g., want, tired) and feelings (e.g., happy, afraid). Recent literature links these social concepts with children's linguistic knowledge (Rice, 1984b).

Concepts, categories, structures, operations, processes, and schemata such as event knowledge are the cognitive and nonlinguistic distinctions that are central to current debates and to the following discussion. The other half of the comparison, language, has also generated its family of terminology and interwoven differentiations.

Language

The major descriptive partitions of language are phonology, grammar (syntax), semantics, and pragmatics. Traditionally, phonology refers to the sounds of a given language; grammar refers to the rules for forming words (e.g., prefixes and endings) and combining words into phrases, clauses and sentences; semantics refers to the way meaning is expressed; and pragmatics refers to the rules for using language in context. Because phonology has not been emphasized in the cognition/language debate, it is not mentioned further.

A major distinction implicit throughout the literature is the contrast between formal syntactic structure and the expression of meaning (semantics). Obviously, the two are not totally separate in that grammatical components can and do convey meaning: e.g., the morphemic unit of final *s* indicates plurality, and the ordering of words (*Mary liked Bill* versus *Bill liked Mary*) conveys who is the agent and who is the object. However, within the perspective of transformational generative grammar, the underlying, abstract rules that account for linguistic structure are regarded as "autonomous and independent of meaning" (Chomsky, 1957, p. 17). According to Chomsky, these rules constitute the linguistic knowledge unique to humans and are what is programmed in the innate, language-specific acquisition device. Chomsky regards the study of syntax to be an important source of insights into the unique nature of human intelligence. Chomsky's emphasis on syntax and explanation is reflected in the assumption of many child language scholars and linguists that syntax is the "real" linguistic knowledge at issue in the discussion of the role of cognition. "Softer" aspects of language, such as word meanings, whose "softness" is a consequence of intrinsically closer ties to meaning, are assumed to be of less importance.

However, a number of linguists have taken issue with Chomsky's partitioning of meaning from grammar. They argued that meanings were part and parcel of the underlying structural rules, at the most basic level (see Newmeyer, 1980, for a clear discussion of contemporary linguistic theories and their origins). The study of case relations or semantic roles, introduced by Fillmore (1968), refers to meanings evident in combinations of words—more precisely, the meaning of the noun phrase in relation to the verb. For example, in the following sentences, the grammatical role of Sue is the same (that of subject), whereas the case relations differ: in *Sue touched Mary*, the notions of agent-action-object are expressed; in *Sue saw Mary*, Sue is an experiencer instead of agent. Grammatical categories based on meanings proved to be well suited to capturing the regularities in children's first word combinations (e.g., Bloom, 1970; Bowerman, 1973; Brown, 1973).

Another aspect of semantics attracted the interest of child language scholars—the acquisition of word meanings. During the 1970s interest in the earliest stages of linguistic understandings led to a concern with the first word meanings and their origins. The involvement with early lexical knowledge coincided with new work interrelating the categorical and lexical structural organization of adults (e.g., Rosch, 1973). The topic continues as a robust area of current investigation.

The observation that children first express linguistic meanings in social context led investigators to explore the pragmatic or sociolinguistic aspects of children's language. Pragmatics encompasses such diverse language-related knowledge as the social functions of an utterance (e.g., assertions, denials, commands), rules for carrying on a conversation, and the use of different speaking styles or registers for different occasions. The earliest precursors of language, the prelinguistic communicative intentions of infants, evident in their gestures and facial expressions, were linked with children's nonlinguistic knowledge and their subsequent linguistic acquisition.

The initial interest in one aspect of children's linguistic knowledge, their mastery of syntactic rules, spread to the associated aspects of semantics and pragmatics. Although these additional dimensions were first seen as sources of explanation for syntactic competence, researchers quickly turned to the study of autonomous semantic and pragmatic competence. Descriptive accounts of their emergence in children's repertoires appeared in the literature along with theoretical explanations of their origins. The totality of children's mental functioning in effect forced investigators to broaden their prospective regarding what is involved in linguistic knowledge.

The comprehensive description of children's linguistic abilities that emerged was consistent with models guiding the work of ethnographers interested in the study of language in its sociocultural context. Hymes (1972) introduced the term "communicative competence," meant to be broadly descriptive of the knowledge that underlies language-in-context. It includes the pragmatic and semantic aspects as well as grammatical structure. Child language scholars adopted communicative competence as an appropriate umbrella term to designate the full range of children's linguistic knowledge. The following discussion of children's language is in the sense of communicative competence. It entails a comprehensive model of children's knowledge of all dimensions of language.

Basic Issues

The question central to much of the contemporary debate is how much of early language acquisition (and the regular, universal patterns) is accounted for by cognition. Given the preceding discussion of what is involved in cognition and language, another way of phrasing the question is: "how do all the pieces of the puzzle fit together?" *Concepts, categories, structures, operations, processes, schemata, event knowledge, syntax, underlying linguistic rules, semantic relations, word meanings, pragmatics*—which of these distinctions illuminate others, or which fit together in identifiable patterns? Some major organizational themes are evident: underlying and surface rules can be distinguished that govern the syntactic, semantic, and pragmatic components of language; processes must be distinguished from structures whether the concern is with cognition or language; the content of cognitive categories must be distinguished from their structure and functions.

The available literature certainly does not represent a systematic or exhaustive investigation of all possible or even reasonable connections among the "pieces" of language and cognition. Each has played a role at one time or another in the questions that have developed during the 1970s. The initial issue was whether or not children's cognitive understanding could account for language acquisition, in a global, all-encompassing sense. Another way of posing this question is to ask whether meaning accounts for language. This question led to others: Does cognition influence only certain aspects of language, such as meanings? Or do available linguistic categories sometimes suggest meanings? This latter question suggests the possibility that the mapping is not always from cognition to language. Methodological issues soon arose as researchers questioned the appropriate level at which to find linkages between cognition and language. What kinds of cognitive knowledge are plausibly linked to which aspects of language? How can these linkages be empirically documented? Finally, researchers focused on the role of mental processes in language acquisition. Are some strategies or principles language specific? If so, are they derived from interactions with the environment, or are they part of the innate mental resources of children? How is cognition implicated in the case of children who are having difficulty acquiring language? Is a language impairment representative of more general cognitive deficits?

These questions reflect the richness and diversity of contemporary competing accounts of the relationship between cognition and language. Current theoretical positions corresponding to these questions are reviewed in the next two chapters. The next chapters present extensions beyond the perspective of Chapters 2 and 3. In Chapter 4 we suggest additional cognitive constructs to include in interpretive models. In Chapters 5 and 6 we shift the focus to development beyond the early stages, to that of school-age children. We provide a summary and concluding remarks in the final chapter.

Chapter 2

Cognition Accounts of Language Acquisition

The decade of the 1970s opened with the promise that underlying meanings—children's cognitive knowledge—could account for the beginnings of language. This possibility was met with enthusiasm and excitement on the part of many investigators. Developmental psychologists were an especially receptive audience for several reasons: Piaget's theories were receiving their first widespread acceptance by American cognitive psychologists in a paradigm triumph over behaviorism; a growing body of evidence regarding the competencies of infants and toddlers suggested that they know far more than previously acknowledged; and the idea simplified language to a system more intuitively graspable than that suggested by the complex abstractions and unfamiliar terminology of existing linguistic models. With a receptive climate, the hypothesis was immediately incorporated into a number of empirical investigations and interpretative accounts. By the mid-1970s the bloom had begun to fade with the appearance of counterarguments. By the end of the decade, a growing body of empirical evidence forced severe restrictions of the original proposals. Furthermore, competing accounts and additional considerations had emerged.

Although initial enthusiasms have diminished considerably, the interest in cognition continues into the 1980s. The contemporary approach is more conservative and constrained. Many current investigations are now patient unravellings of small sections of children's linguistic and nonlinguistic knowledge. There is a renewed interest in other aspects of language acquisition, such as specific linguistic abilities.

The contemporary debate about the relationship between cognition and language has its antecedents in the philosophical and psychological literature. Cromer (1976) and Rieber and Vetter (1980) provided a historical review of this literature. We pick up the debate in the 1970s. Current research addressed the direction of influence and the extent of the linkages between language and cognition. The five major hypotheses can be depicted by modifying Figure 1, as in Figure 2:

1. The solid upward arrow (*A*) represents what is known as the strong cognition hypothesis, the claim that cognitive development accounts for language acquisition.
2. The sets of individual upward arrows (*B*) represent the local homologies account. This is a modification of the strong cognition account that emphasizes the strong contribution of underlying cognition but restricts the influence to localized areas of linkage. These two cognition accounts were dominant in the literature of the 1970s, and are described in this chapter. They inspired the following three counterexplanations of the relationship between language and cognition, which are discussed in Chapter 3.
3. The double-headed arrow (*C*) indicates the interaction explanation, which emphasizes reciprocal lines of influence. Language can sometimes influence cognition, and vice versa.

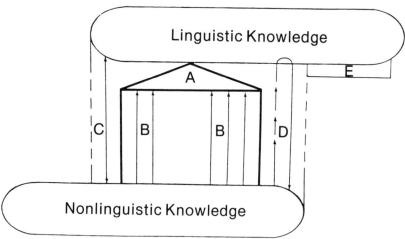

Figure 2 Competing accounts of the cognition/language relationship.

4. The arrow (*D*) that heads upward from cognition toward language in a tentative fashion (broken line), looping through language to return to cognition in a firm manner (solid line) represents the claim that language anchors cognition. In this account, language determines thought by affecting perceptiveness and cognitions.
5. Other accounts have emphasized that some aspects of language are not accounted for by cognition. This weak cognition position is indicated by section *E* of the language domain. Some scholars argue that language-specific processes account for this part of linguistic knowledge that is beyond cognition.

The empirical evidence associated with these positions constitutes a large literature that is expanding rapidly. The following review is selective insofar as it is organized around the develoment of certain explanatory constructs. The reader interested in further information is referred to review chapters by Cromer (1974, 1976, 1981), Bowerman (1978b), Johnston (Note 1), and Bates and Snyder (1982).

Strong Cognition Hypothesis

The *strong cognition hypothesis* (arrow *A* in Figure 2) is rooted in Piaget's belief that language is part of more general mental representational abilities. The emergence of language is contingent on other representational capacities (Piaget & Inhelder, 1969). Given such a perspective, one would expect cognitive knowledge to demonstrate structural parallels to language. The parallel cognitive structures should precede the linguistic ones and be necessary for the development of the linguistic structures.

American psychologists turned to Piaget's account of language acquisition as an alternative to the then-dominant one proposed by Chomsky (1965). Chomsky argued that several striking features of children's language are due to the operation of innate linguistic mechanisms: its rule-governed nature; its rapid, apparently effortless acquisition; and universal regularities in age of acquisition and constraints on linguistic structure. Many scholars were uncomfortable with the idea of specifically linguistic innate mechanisms, especially in the extreme, organic manner in which Chomsky formulated his position. They turned to general cognitive mechanisms as an alternative. Early language as a manifestation of early cognitive development would account for two important phenomena: the universal aspects of acquisition, insofar as early cognitive structures are regarded as universal (a cornerstone of Piaget's theory), and the problem of creativity, the rulegoverned novel utterances of children that proved troublesome for behavioral accounts heavily dependent on imitative processes.

The evidence and arguments associated with the Piagetian perspective appeared simultaneously on three fronts: a description of children's cognitive structures that captured parallels to linguistic structures and meanings; a description of the meanings expressed in children's early language; and an explicit statement of how cognition could account for children's initial mastery of language.

Sinclair (1971; Sinclair–de Zwart 1973), a Genevan scholar, offered an explication of the parallels between early cognitive knowledge and the structure of early language—in particular, the earliest grammatical constructions. In effect, she specified how language could be a reasonable outcome of a child's earlier interactions with his world. Sinclair argued (1971, p. 126) that, prior to his use of language, a toddler can order things temporally and spatially; he can categorize objects according to an action and, conversely, he can categorize actions according to an object; and he can relate object and action to new actions. She pointed out that these cognitive abilities directly parallel the linguistic (grammatical) ones of concatenation, grammatical categories of subject and noun phrase, and the functional grammatical relations of subject and object. Although Sinclair emphasized how prior cognitive achievements allow for children's emerging language, she (1971; Sinclair–de Zwart, 1973) cautioned that the laws of cognitive development alone do not entirely account for language acquisition. An early demonstration of cognitive accomplishments that precede and parallel later linguistic ones is the observation that the strategies young children use when stacking a set of nesting cups follow the same form and order of acquisition evident in children's mastery of grammar, i.e., the structural framework is analogous (Greenfield, Nelson, & Saltzman, 1972).

During this same time, child language scholars turned their interest to the semantics of children's utterances as a framework for accounting for early word order rules. Descriptions of children's first words and word combinations identified a relatively small set of meanings that is remarkably consistent among children in different cultures (Bloom, 1970, 1973; Brown, 1973; Schlesinger, 1971). A striking feature of the meanings is the preponderance of object-related themes, i.e., the fact that objects exist, disappear, and recur, the actions of objects and people, and the location of objects and persons. When children begin to talk, sometime around 12 months of age, half of their first 50 words are names for people or things in their immediate environment, 13% are action words, and 9% are modifiers (Nelson, 1973). Several months later, they begin to combine words. Their first primitive sentences are about the indication of objects (*that ball*), the recurrence of objects (*more juice*), the nonexistence of objects (*allgone ball*), agents and actions (*mommy fix*), actions and objects (*hit ball*), agents and objects (*Mommy pumpkin*, when mother is cutting a pumpkin), agent and location (*baby table*), action and location (*put floor*), and possessor and possession (*Mommy chair*) (examples from Brown, 1973).

These early meanings correspond to Piaget's emphasis on children's interactions with objects as the basis of the cognitive structures that are developed prior to and during the time toddlers are beginning to talk. More specifically, Piaget characterized the first stage of children's intellectual development as the attainment of mental representation, an accomplishment marked by a full understanding of the permanence of objects. Given a close congruity between Piaget's account of mental representation and the dominant meanings of children's first words, it was reasonable to speculate that full mastery of object permanence would be associated with certain linguistic achievements (Bloom, 1973). Two such linguistic correlates of object permanence are the establishment of stable object words (sometimes children's first words disappear after brief usage, to reappear sometime later) and a spurt in vocabulary growth (the first words are usually learned a few at a time, followed by a rapid acceleration in rate of acquisition).

This cognitive hypothesis was fully developed by Macnamara (1972). He argued that cognition is not only *prerequisite to* but also *accounts for* children's linguistic acquisition, at least those aspects of language that express meaning. He specifically acknowledged and excluded the syntactic rules not based on meaning (see p. 6). He asserted that children use their understanding of words to determine semantic structures, and they then note how these structures correlate with the various syntactic devices (p. 7). Put another way, Macnamara proposed that meanings account for children's language acquisition and that such meanings are worked out on a nonlinguistic basis first, in the form of "basic cognitive structures" (p. 11).

The linkage of Piaget's stages of sensorimotor intelligence with language ranged from prelinguistic communicative intentions through children's first words and word combinations. In the prelinguistic period, children are mentally very active. They are busy learning about themselves, other people, and objects in their world.

Piaget described the cognitive achievements of infants and toddlers in six different stages of sensorimotor development. A major accomplishment of Stage Five (sometime around 11 or 12 months) is a primitive use of tools, or a novel means to a familiar goal. An example is the child's ability to pull on a blanket in order to get an object resting on it that is out of reach. This is also the time when children begin to communicate, with primitive requests or statements. Bates (1976) provided examples of Carlotta, observed at 13 months:

> C. is seated in a corridor in front of the kitchen door. She looks toward her mother and calls with an acute sound *ha*. Mother comes over to her, and C. looks toward the kitchen, twisting her shoulders and upper body to do so. Mother carries her into the kitchen, and C. points toward the sink. Mother gives her a glass of water, and C. drinks it eagerly. (p. 55)

This instance illustrates what Bates calls a "protoimperative," involving the child's use of an adult as an agent-tool in obtaining objects. In a similar fashion, young children can use objects as tools to gain attention from adults, in a "protodeclarative." At 12 months, Carlotta purposively seeks and takes an object, such as a picture book, in order to show it to an adult (Bates, 1976, p. 60).

These early communicative behaviors seemed to first appear at the same time as noncommunicative uses of tools, such as tugging on a blanket to get a toy (Bates, 1976; Bates, Camaioni, & Volterra, 1975; Sugarman, 1978). This raised the possibility that children's early verbal communication builds upon a more general mastery of tool use or means to an end, a prediction consistent with Piaget's description of children's mastery of symbols.

Children's first words also reflect what they have worked out nonlinguistically. Clark (1973b) argued that children draw upon perceptual categories such as shape for the formation of their first word categories, which would account for their tendency to use one word, such as *bow-wow*, to refer to more than one animal. On the other hand, Nelson (1974a) proposed that the initial categories were based on actions and relationships. She argued that a word like *ball* is preceded by a concept of ballness that is derived from the actions (rolls, bounces) and relationships (mother throws, picks up) that a child encounters with balls. Both Clark and Nelson presumed that the nonlinguistic concept antedated the word.

Another linguistic achievement that was linked with children's prior cognitive achievements was the transition from single to multiword combinations. It is perplexing that young children often have a number of combinable words in their first vocabulary yet they present them only one at a time. Bloom (1973) and Ingram (Note 2) argued that the apparent constraint was the child's ability to mentally represent more than one notion at a time. Word combinations depended upon this cognitive achievement.

Several things are noteworthy about these early studies: their methodology, the cognitive structure studied, and their heuristic value. Most were descriptions of linguistic or cognitive competence, with accompanying inferences and speculations as to the prerequisite or subsequent competencies in the other domain. Two kinds of cognitive notions were invoked: underlying concepts and categories and deeper, abstract mental structures. More recent studies continued to describe children's early language, particularly word meanings, at a detailed level, whereas other studies included measurements of both language and cognition. Of particular importance are studies that measured Piagetian sensorimotor intelligence and language development, and statistically compared the two.

It is time to reevaluate how the strong cognition hypothesis has fared. The strongest support is at the level of meanings, obtained from descriptions of children's utterances. Slobin (1973, pp. 184–185) suggested that new linguistic forms first are used to express old functions (meanings) and new functions (meanings) first are expressed by old forms. This pattern is consistent with the claim that children start with meanings and look for a way to express them linguistically. An example of new forms for old functions is Brown's (1973) report that children first express their meanings with an unmarked verb, and those meanings later account for the first verb inflections. For example, immediate past is first expressed as *book drop,* and later becomes *book dropped;* intention first as *mommy read,* later as *mommy gonna read.* An example of old forms used for new functions is Cromer's (1976) observation that children used *now* and *yet* in combination with a past tense verb shortly before they acquired the present perfect tense, e.g., an utterance like *I didn't make the bed yet* would appear before *I have not made the bed; now I closed it* would appear before *I have closed it.*

Other aspects of children's acquisition of word meanings support the cognition hypothesis. The fact that children make errors is widely reported (e.g., Kay & Anglin, 1982). They tend to use words in a nonadult manner, suggesting that the words express their own notions and are not rote imitations. A familiar example is a child's use of the word *daddy* to refer to all men. In a similar fashion, children overextend many words. They can also use words in a more restricted way than adults would, such as limiting the word *off* to objects being removed from the body (Bowerman, 1976, p. 135). Children also rely on nonlinguistic strategies for the interpretation of language. For example, when asked to indicate the *top* or *bottom* of an object children show a preference for the upper surface (Clark, 1980). Another observation consistent with conceptual underpinnings of words is that conceptually interrelated words tend to emerge simultaneously. Unlike other word families that appear one at a time, some words are mastered as a set, such as color terms (Bartlett, 1978), markers of current relevance, such as *again, already, yet, still,* and *anymore* (Eisenburg, Note 3), and relational words such as *allgone, bye-bye, back,* and *down* (McCune-Nicolich, 1981a). Finally, children's acquisition of locative terms (*in front of, in back of*) is paced by their nonlinguistic understanding of the spatial relationships between the objects (Johnston, 1979; Levine & Carey, 1982).

The notion of cognitive precursors has not fared well on the level of structural knowledge. Contrary to the early predictions, when investigators compared children's performance on cognitive tasks designed to measure Piagetian structures (such as object permanence, means-end, or symbolic play) with their performance on language tasks, it was found that the cognitive knowledge did not always precede words or word combinations (e.g., Bates, 1979; Corrigan, 1978; Miller, Chapman, Branston, & Reichle, 1980). Object permanence, means-end structures, and symbolic play all are alleged to be the basis for language, yet are not empirically associated with language acquisition. This finding is also confirmed in language-disordered children (Folger & Leonard, 1978).

Local Homologies Hypothesis

The correlational studies do reveal a consistent pattern of association, insofar as cognitive structures and related linguistic knowledge tend to appear at the same time. This pattern led Bates and her colleagues (Bates, 1979; Bates, Benigni, Bretherton, Camaioni, & Volterra, 1977) to propose a *homologue* model, in which both cognition and language are said to derive from a common, deeper underlying system of cognitive operations and structures that is biased toward neither. Because the pattern of cognitive and linguistic linkage is different at different times in development (Bates, 1979), Bates concluded that the homologies are localized, not global (represented by the *B* arrows in Figure 2). That interpretation accounts for the fact that positive correlations between linguistic and cognitive measures are not found at the general levels, such as the attainment of object permanence and the appearance of first words. Instead, positive correlations are found between particular within-stage cognitive tasks and linguistic performances, and those correlations vary across the age range studied.

The local homologies account is a popular modification of the cognition hypothesis because it has evidential and theoretical support (Bates & Snyder, 1982). Complex patterns of correlations are the outcome of virtually every one of the recent studies based on the strategy of administering a battery of cognitive and linguistic tasks. To the extent that different investigators use their own modifications of traditional tasks, variability across studies suggests task-specific relationships. That outcome is predicted by a theory of cognitive development proposed by Fischer (1980), which assumes that in all domains the child acquires skills that are situation specific. Language and cognition are each regarded as a set of overlapping specific skills that are not separate entities but instead interrelate in skill-specific contexts (Fischer & Corrigan, 1981). Therefore, localized linkages between cognition and language are to be expected, as is unevenness in development across skills and skill domains, in part as a consequence of environmental influences. Change in patterns of correlation across time is consistent with skill-specific linkages that emerge in uneven profiles.

Investigators of language-disordered children have found the local homologies account to be helpful. It serves as theoretical support for the conclusion (Leonard, 1979; Morehead & Ingram, 1973) that language-disordered children have a more general representational deficit. Language deficits are but one manifestation of a more pervasive underlying problem. Evidence regarding the cognitive competencies of language-disordered children suggests this position. The close parallels and associations between cognition and language in the development of normal children is also evident in language-disordered children. Just as the language skills of these children are below those of their chronological peers, so are some cognitive abilities, such as imagery (Johnston & Ramsted, 1983; Johnston & Weismer, 1983; Kamhi, 1981), means-end schemes (Leonard & Schwartz, in press), and classification skills (Camarata, Newhoff, & Rugg, 1981; Kamhi, 1981). If depressed language skills are linked with depressed mental representation abilities, it suggests that the latter may be responsible for the former. However, there are grounds for caution.

There is a paradox in the conclusion that language-disordered children have problems with mental representation. The conventional definition of a language-disordered child is a child with the presence of a problem with language acquisition in the absence of

other contributing factors, such as hearing loss, mental retardation, emotional disturbance, or neurological disorder; in other words,
normal development in all but language acquisition. A standard
part of the assessment procedure is the administration of a nonlinguistic intelligence test, in order to establish normal intellectual
development. As Johnston (1982a) and Kamhi (1981) noted, most
of these tests involve tasks that demand some sort of mental representation. Because language-disordered children, by definition,
score within the normal range, there is a problem in interpreting
the mismatch between the intelligence estimates and the deficit in
mental representation implied by the language deficit. Either the
mental representation tasks on the IQ tests are not pervasive or
powerful enough to detect the implied deficit or, to turn the point
around, the nonverbal intelligence tests lead to inaccurate assumptions about language-related cognitive abilities. For example,
Johnson (in press) concluded that Leiter scores for children under
8 years measure children's visual perceptual abilities instead of
their more abstract cognitive knowledge.

Another complication has emerged in recent studies. If the
mental deficits of language-disordered children are linked with
their language performance, we would expect them to perform
below chronological or mental age matches, and commensurate
with language-matched normal children. However, in studies with
mental- and language-matched samples, those expectations are not
always confirmed. For example, Kahmi (1981) reported that on a
classification task language-impaired subjects performed in a manner similar to children matched for mental age. Camarata et al.
(1981) found the performance of language-impaired children on
classification tasks to be poorer than that of children matched for
chronological age, and commensurate with that of those matched
for mean length of utterance (MLU). Leonard and Schwartz (in
press) compared language-impaired subjects with MLU-matched
normal children on several Piagetian measures. They found that
the language-impaired children were consistently below chronological age expectations, but exceeded their MLU matches on
measures of means-end and symbolic play.

Methodological and Interpretative Concerns

The recent expansion of empirical evidence has generated a number of methodological and interpretative questions about the local
homologies hypothesis. Methodological concerns focus on the na-

ture of the evidence. A number of investigators have pointed out the limitations of correlational statistics as a means of unravelling causal relationships. Spurious results can be caused by unidentified covariants, a problem that can be difficult to pinpoint. For example, it is unclear what to make of age as a covariant. Sometimes an apparent relationship between cognition and language disappears when age is partialed out (e.g., Corrigan, 1978, 1979; Miller et al., 1980), and other times it remains (e.g., Quay, Hough, Mathews, & Jarrett, 1981). It may be a function of the age involved, the variance of the measurement tasks, and/or the influence of unidentified abstract cognitive organizational principles. Further complications are imposed by the statistical characteristics of correlations. The stability of the findings depends on a relatively large number of subjects per variable and independent measurement of the variables. These conditions are only partially met in many studies.

Closely related to the problem of statistical inference is the question of how the data are collected. Different methods introduce different biases. Structured assessments and cross-sectional designs are more sensitive to commonalities across children, whereas spontaneous assessments and longitudinal samples are more sensitive to individual differences (Fischer & Corrigan, 1981). Spontaneous samples of language tend to provide a more advanced level of competence than do elicited tasks (Brown, 1973); longitudinal samples, with the opportunity for task familiarity and practice, are more likely to indicate synchrony in development across tasks (and the domains represented) than cross-sectional, once-only measures (Fischer & Corrigan, 1981).

Almost all the studies involving measures of both cognition and language have been based on samples of what the child has mastered in the course of his everyday experiences. An alternative research strategy, less widely used, is a training study, allowing for observation of a child's mastery of the two domains in controlled learning circumstances. Two approaches to training studies investigating cognition and language in young children have been reported. Steckol and Leonard (1981) explored the relationship between means-end schemes (beginning tool use) and relating to objects (socially appropriate use of objects) and prelinguistic performatives (such as the use of an object to get an adult's attention). They trained toddlers on the cognitive tasks and measured subsequent prelinguistic communicative behaviors. The results were mixed: means-end training had no apparent effect, but those children who received training on relating-to-objects schemes increased their use of performatives. However, relating to objects was not directly causally linked to the use of performatives, insofar as two of the four subjects who failed the relating-to-objects tasks also used performatives to communicate.

Another training strategy was used in an investigation of the relationship between underlying categorical knowledge and the acquisition of color words (Rice, 1980). Children's knowledge of color categories was measured prior to training color terms. Those who started training with relevant categorical knowledge tended to learn color terms more easily than those who did not. However, prior categorical knowledge was not a prerequisite for training readiness, insofar as two children without such knowledge also mastered the words easily.

An important advantage of training studies is that they provide a rigorous method for examining cognition/language relationships (see Bates & Snyder, 1982). Their design requires precise task specification and a careful selection of tasks. In order to teach a cognitive or linguistic skill, that skill must be carefully defined: the exact nature of the eliciting conditions must be specified, along with definitions of correct versus incorrect responses. The issue of task selection in training studies is crucial, and draws attention to a fundamental limitation of our present knowledge base. If one is to train either cognitive or linguistic tasks and monitor the other, one must choose an area in which there is reason to believe there are direct linkages across the two domains, at the level of specific skills. These direct linkages are not always obvious in the existing correlational studies.

The identification of target interconnections is central to the cognition/language debate. A range of possible candidates and levels or kinds of cognitive knowledge that can be plausibly linked with linguistic knowledge must be explored. One linkage that can be identified is that of concepts and associated word meanings (Johnston, 1979; Levine & Carey, 1982; Rice, 1980). However, more abstract connections are possible. McCune-Nicolich (1981a) argued that the emphasis on object words as the link with sensorimotor understandings has deflected attention from other candidate linguistic competencies. She reported a longitudinal study of the emergence of relational words, such as *more, allgone, here,* and *up,* and the mastery of sensorimotor constructs. She concluded that children's early meanings of relational words are intimately associated with emerging cognitive operations. Another candidate for connection is the relationship between symbolic play and first word combinations. McCune-Nicolich (1981b) suggested structural parallels between symbolic play and language. Corrigan (1982) reported empirical evidence supporting such parallels. She conducted three studies, one longitudinal and two cross-sectional, with toddlers ages 12 to 28 months. She found a scalable sequence of actor-recipient relationships in pretending, a scalable language sequence, and a significant relationship between the control of actors or recipients in play and the production of animate or inanimate actor-recipients in language. Corrigan emphasized that the comparisons were not in terms of levels of pretend play and language use, but in terms of specific relationships between the two domains based on particular shared skills. Careful task analysis and a match across domains are fundamental to this approach. The possibility that the connections between cognitive operations and language are localized is promising.

A Retrospective Reassessment of Piaget's Contributions

Although the idea of local homologies shares Piaget's emphasis on the driving power of general cognitive mechanisms, current formulations and evidence illustrate some limitations of Piagetian models: Piagetian tasks do not reveal specific linkages of cognition and language; the probability of uneven development across linkages and domains challenges the fundamental Piagetian premise of stage development; and the claim that Piagetian tasks are precursors or covariants of particular linguistic milestones lacks empirical support. Given these conclusions, the contemporary mood is one of reassessment of Piaget's account of early cognitive development as it relates to children's language mastery. A balanced criticism is to be found in the first chapter of Annette Karmiloff-Smith's (1979) book. She is a child language scholar who worked with Piaget and his colleagues at the International Centre for Genetic Epistomology in Geneva. Among other scholars there is a temptation to discard the Piagetian perspective in the wake of more recent insights. Karmiloff-Smith argued that this would be premature.

In contrast to earlier behavioral models, Piaget's account established the active nature of children's mental processes and knowledge. Whereas behaviorists regarded children as passive recipients of environmental influences, Piaget argued that thought develops from a constructive interaction of the child with his environment. The impact of this distinction is evident in the contrast between earlier language therapy procedures based on behaviorism and current methods based on a cognitive approach. In the late 1960s, language training activities were based on elicited imitation, careful specification of stimulus and response, and rigorous schedules of extrinsic reinforcement. Observable behaviors and linguistic forms were the training targets. As the Piagetian model was accepted by language pathologists in the mid-1970s, therapy activities changed to an emphasis on underlying meanings instead of form alone, on spontaneous utterances, and on content matched to a child's cognitive level.

Major conceptual advances have been possible because Piaget's notions corresponded well with many of Chomsky's. Both argued for deep structures (abstract patterns of mental organization that underlie surface regularities in behavior), although they differed as to the origin of the deep structures (a matter discussed in detail in the debate between Chomsky and Piaget, reported in Piatelli-Palmarini, 1980). Both described mental transition mechanisms that act upon experience (i.e., Piaget's operations and structures and Chomsky's transformations). Both detected universal regularities in development. These parallels between two powerful contemporary theorists were noted by other investigators and led to attempts to interrelate the two.

As noted earlier, another valuable contribution was Piaget's characterization of the nature of children's first knowledge, with an emphasis on a child's actions with objects. Such actions are the basis for sensorimotor intelligence, which culminates in the development of mental representation and the use of symbols. The salience of things and actions is also evident in children's first linguistic meanings. Piaget's account offers an interpretation of why this is so, and a means of associating linguistic meanings with a broader cognitive context.

These positive aspects of Piaget's formulations relative to child language are counterbalanced by areas of vulnerability. A major one is a gap in Piaget's stages of cognitive development during the time of most rapid language growth. The first stage, sensorimotor intelligence, accounts for early development, until approximately 18 months. The next stage, preoperational thought, is defined primarily by what the child cannot do: children between 8 months and 7 years have not mastered those concrete operations that appear around age 7 and constitute the third stage of intellectual development. Piaget's account does not capture the nature of the preschooler's rapid mental growth, much of which is linguistic. This relatively empty interval is a consequence of the primary focus of Piaget's goal of explaining the development of formal, logical, scientific thought. Given this perspective, the preschool years (ages 2–6) are some sort of an intellectual backwater, followed by the dynamic flow of forward motion once the gates of rational thought are opened. In contrast, an explanation of language development, which was not Piaget's goal, would emphasize the comparative turbulence of the mental activity during early childhood relative to the apparent calm of later language growth.

Another criticism concerns the nature of the sensorimotor cognitive structures and their alleged causal role in the devleopment of language. Although children's fascination with objects and actions accounts for at least a large proportion of their early linguistic meanings, empirical support for a direct influence on formal linguistic structure in terms of children's emerging grammatical competencies remains to be demonstrated. The heuristic value of sensorimotor structures so far is limited to analogy instead of explanation. On a more specific level, the relevance of Piagetian sensorimotor tasks to language performance is questionable.

Other criticisms form the nucleus of various counterarguments to both the strong cognition and local homologies accounts, arguments that are discussed in Chapter 3. Each is presented in turn, with its associated line of argument and evidence. Briefly, they are:

1. Piaget's account emphasizes only one direction of influence, from cognition to language, ignoring other possibilities.
2. The idea that language is one manifestation of more general cognitive structures, that it serves as a representation of thought, does not take into account that language constitutes a "problem-space" of its own.
3. Piaget's concern with abstract organizational structures overshadowed a recognition of the role of specific mental processes, such as information-getting systems, attention, and memory, all of which are crucial to language acquisition.
4. The conceptual knowledge described by Piaget focused on one kind of category, defined by single attributes, and how such categories can be manipulated by the application of logical principles. That model does not capture other ways children have of conceptually bundling information. Furthermore, these other kinds of concepts and categories have direct parallels in children's linguistic knowledge.
5. Although Piaget did not rule out the importance of social interactions, he underestimated a young child's knowledge of the social world and the contribution of this social understanding to language development.

Chapter 3

Alternatives to the Cognition Account

Both the strong cognition account and the local homologies account assume that children first learn meanings nonlinguistically and that those meanings direct the search for linguistic expression. That assumption has been challenged by a number of scholars. Some scholars take issue with the assumption of a one-way direction of effects and others point out that language entails more than the meanings made available by cognition.

Interaction Hypothesis

The claim that cognition directs early language acquisition is countered by arguments for early bidirectional influence between cognition and language. Proponents of this hypothesis argue that linguistic expressions can alter the nature of children's cognitive development. This alteration arises from an interaction between language and cognition (Arrow C in Figure 2). There are two interpretations of interactive influences. One begins with the child's first utterances, prompted by what he wants to express (underlying meanings). His interlocutors interpret and respond both linguistically and behaviorally to these expressions. This social interaction modifies the child's nonlinguistic meanings and, ultimately, the child's linguistic expression. The other perspective considers the young child as the recipient of others' linguistic formulations. The child becomes aware of certain equivalences (categories) encoded in language that may not have occurred to him on a nonlinguistic basis. The linguistic categories suggest new concepts or modify existing ones, thereby interacting with cognition.

This interactionist position contrasts with the Piagetian account of early language acquisition. Piaget regarded children's first words as symbols for communicating what they already know. Piaget focused on the individual, cognitive sources of knowledge instead of the social context of communication. Piaget seldom discussed the role of the interlocutor in suggesting meanings or offering interpretation. Instead, he described several kinds of behavior as evidence of the attainment of mental representation, such as deferred imitation, symbolic play, and search for hidden objects. The child's personal discovery of mental representation provides him with stored meanings and an appreciation of how symbols can represent them. Such understandings allow a child to look for gestures and, later on, words to express his meanings. In contrast, other scholars, most prominently Vygotsky, emphasized the social context of children's early communication—the contribution of the interlocutor in the development of children's appreciation of words as symbols and their meanings.

Contemporary, microanalytic descriptions of infants' first communications suggest that the beginnings of reference are in the interpretations supplied by others, instead of a child's private, personal cognitive discoveries. Children learn that their behaviors have communicative significance by the reactions of others. For example, children learn that a reaching gesture (one that can appear first as a way of obtaining an object) can function as "I want" by the manner in which their parents respond. The fact that a parent ascribes communicative significance to the gesture suggests to the child that the gesture has meaning (Foster, 1979, Note 4), and the parent's tendency to label the objects indicated by the child's gestures provides linguistic models for the child to use later on (Masur, 1982). In a similar vein, Veneziano (1981) argued that a child's first words emerge in communicative interactions that facilitate the beginnings of symbolic play with objects, an accomplishment that in turn contributes to further word mastery.

Another observation supporting an interaction account is that the nonlinguistic meanings that a child has worked out prior to language are not isomorphic with those encoded in language (Schlesinger, 1977). As was pointed out earlier, the child faces a mapping problem. The regularities of language can provide the clues to solve the problem. As a consequence, linguistic categories suggest new cognitive categories. For example, Schlesinger (1977) argued that our sense of "agentness" is influenced by what our language expresses as an agent. Infants can develop a general notion of agents as they act on things and people in their world and observe others acting in similar ways. This notion is an important one for language. In English, the agent category is marked by word order, evident in such rules as "agent precedes action" (*Mary hit*), and "agent precedes action, which precedes object" (*Mary hit the ball*). In order to apply this rule children must know what is and is not an agent. Schlesinger pointed out that everyday experiences do not provide clear delineations of the boundaries of agentness. "Mummy handing the bottle to the child is no doubt an event where an agent is performing some action, but what about mummy just holding the bottle? To take one further step, can the bottle be said to be an agent 'containing' the milk in the same way that mother is an agent holding the bottle? Clearly there are gradations here of 'agentness'" (p. 156). A similar problem exists for figuring out what constitutes a transitive verb. One possibility is that children notice that the object is affected by the action denoted by the verb (Macnamara, 1972). Schlesinger noted that such general awareness does not answer the question of *how much* the object must be affected if it is to be considered the object of a transitive verb:

> Suppose you hit a wall with your head—is the wall 'affected' without showing it? And when you sit on a bed which has just been made and the bed shows it very much, should it be considered a patient (and hence *sit* as a transitive verb), contrary to what is suggested by the sentence *I sit on the bed?* (p. 157)

Schlesinger concluded that a child's nonlinguistic experience will not automatically provide the distinctions encoded in language. The regularities of language establish the relevant category boundaries, categories that may not have occurred to a child otherwise.

Arguing along much the same lines, other scholars have drawn the same conclusion. Bowerman (1976) provided evidence indicating that early on her daughter used linguistic input as a guide for her own concepts, an argument also proposed by Kuczaj (1982a). Somewhat later in development, children detect subtle regularities in the use of words such as *a* and *the* that suggest similarities in real objects and events (Karmiloff-Smith, 1979), and they use words such as *why* or *how* in order to learn notions that are not readily evident in immediate visual information (Blank, 1974). In a similar vein, Urwin (1982) reported that young blind children use their early linguistic repertoire to work out relationships between objects and persons.

The contemporary interactionist account, introduced as a counter to the cognitive-based explanations, is a strong echo of

Vygotsky's work. In 1934 Vygotsky reasoned that language influences children's thought, within the confines of early concepts: "The language of the environment, with its stable, permanent meanings, points the way that the child's generalizations will take. But, constrained as it is, the child's thinking proceeds along this preordained path in the manner peculiar to his level of intellectual development" (Vygotsky, 1962, p. 68). Vygotsky's prescience is confirmed by the conclusions of modern scholars. For example, on the basis of recent empirical evidence and current models of children's thought, Bowerman (Note 5) concluded that linguistic input in the very early stages of language development activates in the child "a search for the relevant classificational principle(s) from among a somewhat constrained set of candidates."

Although the interactionist account has not been prominent in the training literature, it has important implications for how we regard the problems of language-disordered children and the kinds of remedial activities that are appropriate. The possibility that language influences cognition suggests a different explanation for the poor performance of language-disordered children on some cognitive tasks. If success on nonlinguistic cognitive tasks is facilitated by language, language-impaired children may perform poorly because they lack the problem-solving tools (language) available to normal subjects (Siegel, Lees, Allan, & Bolton, 1981). To the extent that such tests tap distinctions encoded in language, such as *same* and *different*, and language-impaired children do not spontaneously acquire these verbally presented concepts, their cognitive repertoires may be more restricted than those of normal children. If such is the case, it amounts to a reversal of the alleged direction of influence; instead of the language problem being a manifestation of an underlying problem of mental representation, the apparent cognitive limitations would be a consequence of limited ability to extract regularities in linguistic (oral) input.

Even though the interactionist position has not been evident in recent explanations of language disorders, the gist of the argument is implicit in many conventional clinical activities. Indeed, the very nature of the clinical process, in which an adult uses language to teach a child language forms and their associated meanings, presumes that language can interact with and influence children's conceptual understandings. We clinicians assume, as do parents and caretakers, that when we teach a child to say *cup* he recognizes that a set of objects are alike in their cupness, and that he will be able to recognize a novel member of the set on another occasion, even though he may not have had that understanding to begin with. It may be that some of our clinical failures occur when this assumption is false. For example, one of the authors (Rice) was once attempting to teach a youngster the names of colors. After a number of frustrating sessions of limited success, the child asked "Why you call that red?" Obviously, repetitious labeling of the target attribute of objects had not suggested the concept to him. Unfortunately, youngsters are seldom capable of providing such enlightening feedback.

Cognition Anchored in Language

The interaction hypothesis challenges the direction of influence assumed by the strong cognition hypothesis. Schlesinger (1982) argued that the relative strength of the contribution of cognition to language is also questionable. He asserted that language stabilizes cognition by providing a stable inventory of basic categories and operations (Arrow *D* in Figure 2). He observed that, although there are differences across languages in the coding of categories, there is also remarkable similarity. He concluded that this phenomenon is a consequence of the perceptual regularity of the world, a "texture," that "constrains but does not fully determine the formation of concepts" (p. 146). The similarities across languages reflect the constraints; the differences across languages reflect the options within the texture. The texture accounts for children's ease of word acquisition. Schlesinger regarded children's first categories as tentative sortings within the options provided by the perceptual regularities, categories that are "evanescent" in nature. These early categories become permanent when they are "firmly anchored to relatively invariant linguistic responses" (p. 146), i.e., stable categories are a consequence of the convergence of perceptual regularities and linguistic input.

This extension of the interactionist model is also evident in Vygotsky's writing: "The relation between thought and word is a living process; thought is a dead thing, and a thought unembodied in words remains a shadow. The connection between them, however, is not a preformed and constant one. It emerges in the course of development, and itself evolves" (1962, p. 153).

In the modern period, the claim that language determines thought is most closely identified with what has come to be known as the "Whorfian hypothesis" after linguist Benjamin Lee Whorf (1956, first published in 1940). Whorf was concerned with the influence a native language has on the perceptions and thoughts of individuals within a particular society. He argued that the differences across languages in semantic and grammatical distinctions lead to differences in thought; that one's native language shapes one's intellectual experiences. The appeal and durability of this idea is evident in recent remarks of Jerome Kagen's (1982) regarding the emotions of infants and adults. He argued that infant fear is qualitatively different from adult fear, contrary to common assumptions. He attributed what he regarded as a cultural misconception to the influence of language:

> In many cultures, adults use different words to describe what seem to be similar characteristics in adults and young children. In Japanese, for example, there are different words for intellectual ability in adults and infants. I suspect that one reason that Americans have such a strong faith in the continuity of human qualities is that English uses the same terms for infant, child, and adult qualities. Using the same words to describe the characteristics of a baby and an adult convinces you that you are talking about the same quality. (p. 54)

A major question about the Whorfian account is the extent to which a group's language influences their thoughts. Does their language determine their concepts (what is regarded as a strong interpretation), or merely predispose them to think in one way or another (a weak interpretation)? Both interpretations rest upon an important assumption: the world offers a variety of phenomena that can be arbitrarily divided up as a given group of language users sees fit. To the extent that the world offers ready-made structures that have psychological utility for all speakers, one would expect to find those cognitive predispositions directing language instead of vice versa.

Investigators of Whorfian issues have focused on color categories. Different linguistic cultures have different numbers of color words—some have only a few whereas others, such as English, have many. It has been commonly assumed that these cross-linguistic differences reflected flexibility of the color spectrum; as a continuum of light variations it could be arbitrarily divided at different points by different cultural groups. If it is true that one's language shapes one's perceptions, then speakers should be sensitive to those color differences encoded in their own language and overlook color boundaries in other languages.

This hypothesis has been refuted in the worl of Eleanor Rosch (1973; Rosch & Mervis, 1975; summarized by Brown, 1978), along with the assumption that the color spectrum can be chunked into bundles in whatever way a speaker chooses. Rosch demonstrated that the color continuum is psychologically organized around perceptually salient, focal colors (a finding consistent with physiological evidence of how the human vision apparatus is structured; Bornstein, 1973. Regardless of whether or not a language has a name for *red*, people agree that a focal red (a true red) is a better example of redness than a peripheral red (an orangish red). Furthermore, even for speakers of languages lacking the names for focal colors, the labels for focal colors are learned first and remembered most readily. Gaps in the native speakers' lexicon do not limit their ability to learn color terms, thereby refuting the notion of linguistic determinism. In addition to color, geometric shapes (Rosch, 1973) and natural objects (Rosch, Mervis, Gray, Johnson, & Boyes-Braem, 1976) have universal regularities in their internal conceptual structure, despite external linguistic differences.

The contemporary interaction account of the relationship between children's thoughts and their language differs from the Whorfian hypothesis in the acknowledgment of the inherent organization of nature and children's sensitivity to naturally occurring regularities. Schlesinger (1982) used the metaphor of texture; Bowerman (Note 5) suggested inherent constraints on the classificational principles available to children. Another difference is the contemporary acknowledgement that some thoughts resist expression in language, something relatively overlooked in the Whorfian account. Schlesinger recognizes the plasticity of early thought and the role of language in shaping early cognitive categories, a matter addressed in detail by Vygotsky in earlier writings.

If language stabilizes concepts, the status of thought in children who do not acquire language, or who do so in an unusual manner, is questionable. Are their thoughts qualitatively different from those of normal speakers? Do they lack the concepts encoded in language, or are their notions less stable than those of normal speakers? Deaf children who have learned neither speech nor sign language are naturally occurring cases of cognitive development in the absence of language. Although their intellectual development has been extensively studied, the findings are inconclusive (Ottem, 1980; Quigley and Kretschmer, 1982). A variety of cognitive assessments have been used in studies, including Piagetian measures, categorization tasks, and problem-solving paradigms. Furth (1966), reporting on a series of studies designed to determine whether language is essential to the development of Piagetian structure, concluded that "language does not influence development in any direct, general, or decisive way" (p. 160). Yet he did acknowledge that language may have specific influence, insofar as it furnishes symbols appropriate for specific situations. The performance of deaf children on "certain specific tasks in which available word symbols or linguistic habits facilitate solution" (p. 160) may be retarded. Furth's characterization of the deaf as cognitively comparable to hearing persons was in response to the then-dominant Whorfian-inspired characterization of hearing-impaired persons as qualitatively different from their hearing peers. Although Furth's work has not proved to be definitive (see critiques by Cohen, 1977, and Moores, 1978), his primary conclusion has been widely accepted.

Contemporary research has focused on methodological issues, such as the problem of ambiguous instructions for deaf children and the possible role of mediation by a language code other than the standard oral verbal one. In many of the earlier studies it was assumed that, if children were deficient in verbal language, they did not use any other language codes, such as sign, to mediate the tasks; to the extent that other systems were actually available, the language-cognition distinction is obscured. The current picture of the cognitive competencies of the deaf is complex (Quigley & Kretschmer, 1982). Given clear instructions, they readily learn preconceived concepts in structured situations, but seem to have difficulty with spontaneous flexibility. Deaf children's progress through the early Piagetian stages and structures is roughly parallel to that of hearing children, although some tasks, such as conservation, can prove troublesome; the extent to which they master formal operations is unclear.

In short, one general issue seems to be resolved: children who do not have access to the standard, verbal language of their culture nevertheless think much like their speaking peers; in the general sense, then, language is not necessary for cognition. An equally important conclusion is that, in specific cases, words and linguistic structure do exert influence on thought. The notion of specific, as opposed to general, influences is consistent with the local homologies account presented earlier and with the interaction hypothesis. The problem that remains is how to characterize the specific areas of linguistic influence. Methodological complexities inherent in work with hearing-impaired children (or any children with language limitations) impose special difficulties. The problem of task instruction is an initial hurdle; a more basic dilemma is the specification of what constitutes "verbal" as opposed to "nonverbal" knowledge, especially at the level of formal operations.

The work with hearing-impaired persons and the notion of language as an anchor to cognition brings us to an intimately related issue, that of the use of language as a tool in thinking. We defer a discussion of verbal mediation and similar matters to Chapter 5.

Weak Cognition Hypothesis

The preceding hypotheses have focused on the close association of underlying cognition and the expression of meaning in language. Other authors point out that, even if cognition accounts for meanings, this does not entail an account of all of language. Johnston and Slobin (1979) illustrated the problem with a "waiting room metaphor." It is as if the child can enter a waiting room associated with each linguistic form. Entrance is gained by the acquisition of a concept underlying language. While in the waiting room the child must figure out how to express the notion in language. The solution requires various amounts of time and effort, depending on the linguistic form. In this metaphor, cognition provides only the initial entry into language (the notions to be conveyed)—it does not provide the particulars of linguistic rules (the semantic and morphosyntactic distinctions involved). This position has been identified as the *weak cognition hypothesis* (Cromer, 1976). To return to our schematic representation of the mapping problem, the concern is with the kinds of linguistic knowledge not accounted for by cognition (section *E* of Figure 2).

Observations in support of this position center on two facts about language: (1) some aspects of grammar are arbitrary, not derived from or consistent with distinctions of meaning; and (2) there are different ways to say the same thing, different syntactic formulations to express the same meanings. This is the case within a particular language, and is also evident across languages, in the different conventions for expressing particular meanings.

In the earlier discussion of the mapping problem we mentioned a few examples of arbitrary grammatical conventions not based on meaning. The manner in which children master these conventions indicates that they draw upon more than their nonlinguistic knowledge base. There are a number of examples of language acquisition independent of meaning, among which are the following. First, children learn new, more linguistically complicated ways of expressing the same notion. A case in point is how they acquire self-reference. They first refer to themselves by proper name, then later by *I* or *me* in the proper grammatical contexts, a transition that cannot be accounted for by a shift in underlying meanings. Second, children acquire grammatical restrictions that operate on the expression of meanings, such as those involved in the word pairs *sold/bought*, *pour/fill*, and *ask/tell*. Their errors indicate that they have mastered the nonlinguistic notions, the underlying meanings, but are still sorting out the formal linguistic devices available for the expression of the meanings (e.g., Bowerman, 1982a; Chomsky, 1970). Third, sometimes children start with the formal intralinguistic relationships and then work backward toward the meanings. For example, they first use color terms as a response to the question *What color is this?*, and later work out the relationship between the color properties of objects and their corresponding color terms (Bartlett, 1978). In other words, they first realize that the word *color* subsumes a group of words, such as *red* or *green*, and subsequently figure out what *red* means.

The second feature of language, the fact of different ways to say the same thing, is evident in such pairings as *He loves Mary* versus *He is fond of Mary*. The meanings are equivalent but the grammatical structure is not; the notion of affection is grammatically represented as a verb in *loves* and as a copular and adjective construction for *is fond of*. Maratsos and Chalkley (1980) cited this example as counterevidence to the claim that children can use underlying meanings (semantics) as a direct route to grammar. Instead, children must simultaneously cope with meanings and formal structures.

Another perspective on the problem of how to match meanings with grammatical options is evident in cross-linguistic studies. Slobin (1973, 1982) suggested that cross-linguistic differences allow for the inference of language-processing principles that are independent of cognition. Observation of children learning different languages allows for a determination of which linguistic patterns are easiest to master. The assumption is that all children start with the same set of meanings to express. The lag between the first attempts to communicate certain meanings and the mastery of the relevant linguistic devices, which vary across different languages, would then serve as a rough index of linguistic complexity. The strategy can be schematically represented in a modification of the mapping design (Figure 3).

Slobin's (1973) test case for the strategy involved the acquisition of locative terms in two languages, Hungarian and Serbo-Croatian. Toddlers simultaneously learning both languages learned to express notions of location, such as *into, out of, onto,* and *on top of,* in Hungarian some time before they did so in Serbo-Croatian. A comparison of the two languages revealed the reason: the Hungarian means of expressing location is simpler than the grammatical complexities of Serbo-Croatian. The manner in which the two languages differ allows for the inferences of linguistic processing strategies, such as "pay attention to the ends of words."

The work with locatives has been extended to a comparison of the acquisition of locatives in English, Turkish, Serbo-Croatian,

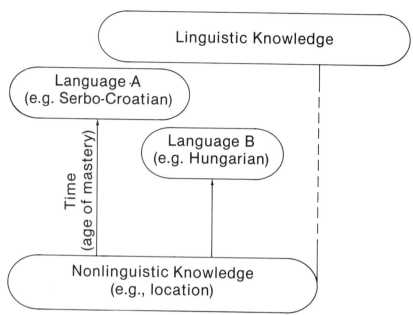

Figure 3 Slobin's strategy for the inference of linguistic processing strategies.

and Italian (Johnston & Slobin, 1979; Slobin, 1982). Five linguistic factors contribute to the relative difficulty of learning locatives in English and Serbo-Croatian versus Turkish and Italian:

1. Turkish locatives, unlike those in the three Indo-European languages, are inserted after the noun.
2. Turkish and Italian have only single lexical items for each relation, whereas English and Serbo-Croatian have multiple terms such as *next to, beside, by, near,* and *close to.*
3. The languages vary in the clarity of the locative terms to nominals that name the location or corresponding body part.
4. The languages vary in the morphological complexity of the locatives, from single morphemes like *on* to multimorpheme expressions such as *on top of.*
5. The languages vary in the extent of homonymity present.

Cognition determines a relatively stable order for the acquisition of locative terms across the languages: *in, on, under,* and *beside* are acquired earlier than *between, back,* and *front.* However, there are language-specific departures from this order because of the interaction of the five linguistic factors.

Other evidence that cognition and language are not necessarily synchronous comes from atypical children. Such children provide crucial documentation of dissociations between cognition and language that are obscured by the patterns of normal development. During the time of language acquisition normal children are also changing rapidly in other areas. They are growing intellectually, socially, and physically as well as communicatively. Because of the simultaneity of acquisition across domains, it is difficult to sort out whether two aspects, such as cognition and language, are linked or whether their coappearance is a function of more general common developmental mechanisms. For example, Roberts and Corbitt (Note 6) reported a high correlation between change in shoe size and development of classification skills in 2–7-year-olds. Such apparent "relationships" attest to the fact that youngsters grow and change simultaneously across disparate aspects of development. An important supplement to the many studies that rely on correlation between cognitive and linguistic measures as an index of the association of the two is the description of special cases of development in which language and cognition are independent. Most revealing are the cases where linguistic competencies remain intact while cognitive abilities are diminished or impaired. In order for this to occur, linguistic functioning must have some autonomous mental structures. A number of such instances have been reported:

1. Mentally handicapped children's linguistic ability can sometimes exceed their general cognitive functioning (Miller, 1981), a finding inconsistent with the idea that cognition constrains language.
2. Likewise, some children who demonstrate complex grammatical structures perform poorly on measures of mental representation, classification, hierarchical organization, and conservation, all cognitive abilities that have been hypothesized as necessary for language (Curtiss, 1982; Curtiss, Kempler, & Yamada, Note 7; Curtiss, Yamada, & Fromkin, Note 8).
3. Another finding that suggests language-specific factors is that aphasic children who are unable to express themselves with verbal language can be taught to express their ideas with nonlinguistic symbols (Cromer, 1981, pp. 73–74).

Language-specific Processes

The conclusion that cognition does not account for all of language leads directly to the question of how the formal aspects of language are acquired. If children's language acquisition is at least somewhat distinct from their general understandings and cognitive processing mechanisms, what else is involved? The obvious candidate is some sort of specifically linguistic processing ability, a particular set of skills available to very young children. The detection and description of language-specific acquisition strategies is the goal of Slobin's cross-linguistic developmental comparisons and the work of Curtiss and her colleagues, documenting the kinds of linguistic knowledge that are dissociated from general cognitive abilities. However, before proceeding further, we must note that the belief that language constitutes a unique "problem space" for children does not entail the conclusion that language-specific mental mechanisms are involved. Karmiloff-Smith (1979), for instance, argued that children apply general problem-solving structures to the linguistic "problem space." The existence and nature of language-specific processes and how they are to be differentiated from other mental abilities are the focus of current research and debate.

One possibility is some sort of innate mental mechanisms particularly evolved for and suited to language acquisition, an idea proposed earlier by Chomsky (1965) and by Lenneberg (1967). Essentially, the claim is that language acquisition is a matter of the maturational unfolding of biologically given linguistic competencies, an unfolding triggered by social interactions and environmental experiences. This hypothesis was out of fashion among child language scholars during the 1970s, but it has recently reappeared. The currency of innatism is evident in a series of debates between Chomsky and Piaget that were held in France in 1975 (Piatelli-Palmarini, 1980). Chomsky (1980) specified that the "language faculty" that is biologically programmed is the computational aspect, defined as the rules of phonology, syntax, morphology, and certain semantic structures. What he regards as the conceptual components of language, such as object reference and thematic, pragmatic, and real-world knowledge, are not included in the "language faculty."

Cromer (1981) has recently reformulated his position on language acquisition to include the possibility of innate factors. He proposed an *epigentic-interactionist viewpoint* (1981, pp. 90–102). He asserted that "there is inherent in the human species a number of unfolding developmental phenomena, some of which may be specifically linguistic, that interact with environmental variables" (1981, p. 90). He emphasized that he does not claim that particular linguistic structures are necessarily innate (as does Chomsky), but instead that innate potential interacts with environmental factors in the development of structures. He avoided a strong claim that there are "specifically linguistic" innate processes, but argued that there is good reason to consider the possibility. Macnamara (1982) also allowed for language-specific faculties in his recent discussion of children's acquisition of names for things.

One reason for the appeal of innate language-specific mechanisms is their usefulness in accounting for universal regularities in the acquisition of linguistic structures. There are remarkable commonalities across children and cultures in the age and apparent ease of acquisition. Furthermore, there are similarities across languages in the structures that are acquired and the sequence of appearance, and the structures that are *not* evident, even though they are logically possible.

Linguistic commonality is most striking in the case of creole languages. Children whose parents speak an early-stage pidgin language (a simple language blending two different languages) learn a creole language, a more complex version of the pidgin language. Bickerton (1981, 1982) pointed out that these children learn a language not known by their parents (who speak a native language and a pidgin). Moreover, their creole rules and features are much like those invented by other creole speakers by time and distance.

Bickerton argued that similar principles regulate the acquisition of language by children and the emergence of creole languages from preceding pidgin language. A pidgin language is markedly limited in its inventory of morphological devices and syntactic forms. Bickerton argued that successive generations introduce cumulative innovations into the pidgin that eventually result in the emergence of creole language that is replete with a wide range of morphological devices and syntactic forms. Children introduce novel yet systematic grammatical rules into the pidgin during the process of creolization. Bickerton argued:

> It violates both parsimony and common sense to suppose that children use one set of acquisition strategies for 'normal' acquisition situations, and then switch to another set when they find themselves in a pidgin-speaking community: parsimony because two explanations would be required where one should be adequate, and common sense because there is no way a child could tell what kind of community he has been born into, and therefore no way he could decide which set of strategies to use. (1981, p. 6)

The solution to this dilemma is to assume that both language acquisition and creolization are regulated by a common "bioprogram." This bioprogram is evident in parallels between language acquisition and creolization in five primary domains: the emergence of definite versus indefinite articles; the use of verbal auxiliaries for state versus process verbs; the marking of punctual versus nonpunctual aspect; a preference for causative rather than inchoative (noncausative) constructions; and the acquisition of sentential complements, movement rules, and subject relative clauses. An example familiar to most students of child language revolves around the acquisition of the English progressive marker *-ing*. As has been frequently noted, although children commonly overgeneralize *-ed* (producing *comed, goed,* or *eated*), they do not overgeneralize *-ing* to stative verbs such as *like, want,* or *know* but do overgeneralize it to nonstative nouns like *weather,* producing *weathering* (Kuczaj, 1978).

Bickerton argued that the state-process distinction is an elemental part of the innate language bioprogram. As such, it plays a critical role in the process of creole formation. In creoles, the stative-nonstative distinction is regularly observed by the emergent verbal auxiliary system. For example, in the Hawaiian Pidgin English (HPE) of pre-1920 immigrants, auxiliary verbs for marking tense, modality, and aspect are largely absent. Yet in Hawaiian Creole English (HCE) of locally born speakers, auxiliaries are common. In particular, *stei* is used prior to a verb to mark nonpunctual, continuous, or habitual actions or events. *Stei + verb* is not used to mark isolated, nondurative actions or events. In HPE, *stei* is used as a locative main verb as in *mi iste nalehu tu yia* (i.e., "I was in Nalehu for two years") (Bickerton, 1981, p. 26). In HCE, *stei* is used as a free-standing, preverbal auxiliary as in *ai no kea hu stei hant insai dea, ai gon hunt* ("I don't care who's hunting in there, I'm going to hunt") (p. 28). *Stei* never occurs with stative verbs.

Such parallels between language acquisition and creolization suggest, to Bickerton, that both are determined by an innate bioprogram that specifies a common set of conceptual distinctions that are typically marked by linguistic distinctions. A genetic program for language unfolds as part of the normal development of each child. This bioprogram specifies a core set of conceptual and linguistic distinctions that are overlaid by both formal universals and language-specific grammatical rules. Language acquisition consists in modifying and adapting the core bioprogram to fit the exigencies of the modern adult language. Creolization consists in using the bioprogram to remedy deficiencies in the input pidgin language.

A reconsideration of language-specific mental processes is consistent with a renewed interest in organic factors associated with language acquisition. The most firmly established evidence of biological specialization is in the case of speech perception. Many scholars accept the conclusion that phonetic perception is distinctly linguistic, an innate auditory faculty that is made to conform to

the acoustic consequences of the way speech movements are produced (Liberman, 1982). Other investigators are working to bridge
contemporary advances in developmental neurology with language function and dysfunction (such as the group at the University of California, Los Angeles: Curtiss et al., Note 8; Fromkin,
Note 9). A third approach to organic factors is the current work in
behavioral genetics. Recent findings (Hardy-Brown, Plomin, & De
Fries, 1981; Hardy-Brown, Note 10) suggest particular genetic influences on children's early language acquisition. Fifty adopted
1-year-old children were studied. Their communicative abilities were
assessed and compared with the cognitive abilities of their birth
mothers and their adoptive mothers. The relationships between
the infants and their birth mothers were more pervasive than between them and their adoptive mothers. In particular, the birth
mother's memory abilities were associated with a number of aspects of the infant's communicative development.

The work in speech perception, developmental neurolinguis-
tics, and behavioral genetics portends an enhanced credibility for
the possibility that specific linguistic abilities contribute to children's language acquisition. Whereas the notion of a "language
acquisition device" was widely regarded as outrageously implausible during the 1970s, it shows signs of restored respectability in
the 1980s.

If cognition does not fully account for language, and other
processes are involved, how are we to regard the nature of the
problems of children manifesting language disorders? To the extent that language is independent of general mental representation
mechanisms, a language disorder is not necessarily evidence of an
underlying deficit in mental representation. Instead, it may indicate deficits in specific processes that may or may not be unique
to language, mental processes that are overlooked in the Piagetian
framework. Cromer (1981) argued that language disorders involve
deficits in processes such as short-term memory, auditory processing, auditory storage, and hierarchical planning. He reviewed a
number of studies in which such deficits are reported in children
with language disorders, as did Johnston (1982a). The possibility
that language disorders are the consequence of a perceptual
processing deficit has been a traditional and controversial issue in
the speech pathology literature (see Lubert, 1981; Rees, 1973; Tallal, Stark, Kallman, & Mellits, 1981). Although such difficulties
may be evident in the performance of language-disordered children, their causal significance has yet to be established: they may
coexist with the language difficulties as an unrelated problem; they
may both be surface manifestations of a deeper problem; limited

linguistic competence may inhibit performance on some perceptual tests, or on intervening variables such as selective attention; or the influence of perceptual processes may be evident on only certain aspects of language, or under particular circumstances, such as elicited language tests, fatigue, or the presence of competing stimuli.

A return to an innatist or a perceptual processing account of language acquisition has some unsettling implications for language rehabilitation. Butterfield and Schiefelbusch (1981) mentioned several. One is that an emphasis on internal factors diminishes the role of the environment. A basic assumption of training is that by altering a child's environment we can enhance linguistic acquisition. Another implication concerns what to teach. If the child's basic difficulty is at the process level, a direct approach to remediation of the problem is to teach those processes. However, that strategy has been tried and found to be wanting (Butterfield & Schiefelbusch, 1981, p. 174).

To the extent that specific processes hypotheses suggest a pessimistic outlook for remediation, they require conservative criteria for acceptance. However, the problems are not limited to this account of acquisition. They are also inherent in the view that regards language as one manifestation of mental representation. The question of what to teach applies there as well; the kinds of representation or cognitive knowledge to be taught are not self-evident, nor are the criteria for mastery (see Rice, 1980, pp. 154–160). Furthermore, the effectiveness of cognitive training at the level of mental representation for the purpose of language acquisition remains to be established.

On the other hand, it would be unproductive to rule out the possibility of innate factors. As an explanatory concept, an innate hypothesis is not necessarily pessimistic. Insofar as children with language difficulties can learn language in a manner parallel to normal acquisition, they serve as evidence of the relative robustness of human language-learning capacities. Contrariwise, if differences in linguistic structure can be identified relative to normal acquisition, they would contribute to the specification of particular language-specific mechanisms of learning. So far, the search for deviant linguistic structure has been unfruitful (Rice, 1978), but the possibilities are far from exhausted. For example, Johnston and Kamhi (Note 11) investigated performance across linguistic domains, comparing syntactic and semantic variables in the utterances of normal and language-impaired children. They reported that language-impaired children produced fewer logical propositions per utterance and indicated less control of formal syntactic markers. Their findings suggest asynchronous development across linguistic domains in the case of language-impaired children. Problems with the interface of syntax and semantics are heretofore undetected subtleties in the linguistic patterns of children who have difficulty with language acquisition. Further investigation at this level of description may clarify some of the linguistic processes that are involved in language acquisition of both disordered and normal children.

The ideas that internal processing factors influence language acquisition also has clinical utility. Cromer (1981, pp. 124–127) linked this perspective with one of the basic axioms of therapy, a recognition of individual differences. Knowledge of each child's perceptual, cognitive, and linguistic constraints is essential for effective remediation. The recent recognition of cognitive factors has balanced the earlier enthusiasm for behaviorism, in that it has returned the clinical focus to the internal capacities of children as well as environmental events. An open mind in regard to language-specific processes may reduce to the simple observation that children vary in their linguistic aptitude, and the extreme extent of limitation may be most evident in the case of particular language-disordered children.

Overview of Competing Accounts

For an overview of the various accounts of the relationship between nonlinguistic knowledge and language we can return to Figure 2. The major aspects in dispute are the direction of influence, the location and the extent of linkage, and the kind of linguistic knowledge to be accounted for. Among the issues embedded in the debate are the definitions of language and cognition, the existence of linguistic universals and linguistic relativism, the nature and origins of early symbolic representation, organic influences on language acquisition, and the nature of language dysfunction. Given such an array of unresolved issues, it is no surprise that the debate continues to be vigorous.

A further perspective can be gained from Table 1. The distribution of supporting evidence reveals that the different explanations tend to focus on different levels of linguistic competence, and on different kinds of linguistic phenomena. Accounts that emphasize the influence of cognition are centered on the earlier stages of acquisition, whereas explanations that emphasize linguistic influence or uniqueness concentrate on later stages. Hypotheses based on cognition deal with the linguistic expression of

Table 1 Summary of Evidence Associated with Explanations of the Cognition/Language Relationship

Prelinguistic	Appearance of Words and Word Combinations	Later Language Development
I. Strong Cognition Hypothesis: Cognition preceeds and accounts for language acquisition		
	New forms; old functions, e.g., first verb inflections encode concepts expressed earlier in unmarked verbs (Brown, 1973).	Old forms; new functions—e.g., *now* and *yet*—are used in combination with a past tense verb to make present perfect shortly before the acquisition of perfect tense.
	Children make errors in the use of words (e.g., Kay & Anglin, 1982).	Conceptually interrelated words tend to emerge as a set (e.g., Bartlett, 1978; McCune-Nicolich, 1981a; Eisenberg, Note 3).
	Children use nonlinguistic strategies for the interpretation of language (e.g., Clark, 1973a; 1980).	Acquisition of locative terms (*in front of*, *in back of*) is paced by their nonlinguistic understandings (Johnston, 1979; Levine & Carey, 1982).

II. Local Homologies Hypothesis: Simultaneous emergence of parallel cognitive and linguistic knowledge

Piagetian Stage 5 performance in causal understanding, means-end relations, and object schemes appears with the development of prelinguistic intentional vocal and gestural signals, although not in a certain order (e.g., Bates, 1979).

Training relating to objects schemes tends to an increase in the use of performatives, whereas training on means-end does not affect performatives (Steckol & Leonard, 1981).

Communicative behaviors of Down's syndrome children generally correspond to their sensorimotor levels of performance (Greenwald & Leonard, 1979).

Comparisons of object permanence and linguistic measures yield variable results—they tend to appear at the same time but not in a certain order; the relationship may disappear with age partialed out (e.g., Corrigan 1978, 1979).

Similar variability is reported in comparisons of means-end and linguistic measures (e.g., Bates, 1979; Folger & Leonard, 1978; Siegel, 1981).

Comprehension of language correlates with sensorimotor performance, but sensorimotor measures do not predict language comprehension with age partialed out (Miller et al., 1980).

Structural parallels are evident between symbolic play and language acquisition (Corrigan, 1982; McCune-Nicholich, 1981b).

Children with reduced linguistic competence perform below chronological age expectations on cognitive tasks, such as imagery (Kamhi, 1981; Johnston & Ramsted, 1983), means-end schemes (Snyder, 1978), mental representation (Leonard & Schwartz, in press), and classification (Camarata et al., 1981; Kamhi, 1981).

Cognitive variables contribute to communication skills independent of age and socioeconomic status of 7–9-year-olds (Quay, et al., 1981).

Table 1 (continued)

Prelinguistic	Appearance of Words and Word Combinations	Later Language Development
III. Interaction Hypothesis: Language and cognition mutually influence each other's development		
Children attribute communicative significance to gestures, such as reaching, as a consequence of mother's interpretation (Foster, 1979, Note 4).	The emergence of first words and symbolic play with toys interact in a reciprocal fashion (Veneziano, 1981). The categories do not necessarily correspond to ones that children are likely to have worked out nonlinguistically; children must adjust their concepts to conform to those of their native language (Schlesinger, 1977). Some of the concepts governing children's first words are suggested by linguistic input (Bowerman, 1976, p. 136; Kuczaj, 1982a).	In some cases, words appear before meanings, and can serve as clues to meanings, e.g., children use words like *why* or *how* before they understand them, in an apparent search for meanings (Blank, 1974); children's use of determiners, such as *a* and *the*, can suggest conceptual distinctions, such as the set of nouns (things) versus verbs (nonthings) (Karmiloff-Smith, 1979, p. 235).
IV. Cognition-anchored-in-language Hypothesis: Children's concepts are unstable until anchored with linguistic forms.		
		Languages tend to encode the same concepts, yet there are differences that children must adjust to; the similarity across languages is a consequence of the perceptual regularities in the world (texture), which constrain but do not fully determine categories (hence, the possibility of differences); children's first concepts are tentative sortings within the textural patterns, which become anchored when attached to relatively invariant linguistic responses (Schlesinger, 1982).

V. Weak Cognition Hypothesis: Cognition does not account for all language development

Mentally handicapped children's linguistic ability can sometimes exceed their general cognitive functioning (Miller, 1981).

Aphasic children can be taught to express in a nonlinguistic mode concepts that were not acquired linguistically (Cromer, 1981, pp. 73–74).

Some atypical children who demonstrate complex grammatical structures perform poorly on allegedly parallel cognitive tasks (Curtiss et al., Notes 7, 8).

Children learn new, more linguistically complicated ways of expressing the same notion; for example they first learn to refer to themselves by name, followed by incorrect then correct use of I/me (Cromer, 1976).

Children must learn the interactions between word meanings and grammatical restrictions—e.g., children make errors with pairs such as sold/bought, pour/fill (Bowerman, 1982a), and ask/tell (Chomsky, 1970), as a function of grammatical context; children sometimes first learn words as a response to other words, later as reference to meanings—e.g., color terms are first learned as a response to "What color is this?" (Bartlett, 1978).

VI. Mental processes not rooted in meanings: Language-specific and/or perceptual processes

There are universal regularities in the age and pattern of acquisition as well as cross-linguistic commonalities in linguistic structures present and not present (even though logically possible) (Chomsky, 1965; Cromer, 1981).

Children learn a creole language not spoken by their parents; creole languages separated by time and space share common features (Bickerton, 1981, 1982).

Language disorders are associated with problems in perceptual processing and/or memory (for reviews see Johnston, 1982a, and Cromer, 1981).

meanings; noncognition accounts involve formal properties of what does and does not appear in linguistic structures. An obvious conclusion is that the relationship between cognition and language may vary as a function of age, linguistic abilities in question, and type of cognition involved (see Schlesinger, 1977, pp. 166–167). If that is the case, any attempt to characterize the relationship in global terms is misdirected.

Another striking characteristic of the literature is the preliminary, tentative character of the available evidence and the associated arguments. The methodological challenges of studies with very young children push the limits of contemporary behavioral science. One obvious problem is the need for independent measures of cognitive and linguistic knowledge. Many of our assumptions about what children know apart from and prior to language are based on inferences from how they use language. Language-based measures of cognition imply a circularity in our reasoning about the role of cognition in language acquisition. This methodological concern is especially relevant when working with children who do not use language. In this case, it is difficult to determine whether such children lack the underlying cognition or lack the means to express what they know, or, to put it another way, whether they have little to talk about or have ideas and concepts they are unable to express (see Rice, 1980, pp. 17–39).

Given that the issue is more complex than initially supposed and the available scientific methods are crude relative to the task, how is the literature to help those who work with language-disordered children? Two conclusions can be drawn, at different levels of concern. On the level of explanation, the existing debates form a context for how we regard the nature of a language problem. There is a temptation to cast all cases of language impairment as a consequence of one common causal factor. However, the diversity of explanations suggests a diversity of contributing factors as well; some children's problems may be a consequence of one limitation, whereas other limits operate in other cases, or different patterns may be involved across children. Such possibilities would focus on the heterogeneity of language-disordered children instead of the assumption of homogeneity, and would move theoretical formulations toward clinical reality.

On the level of remediation activities, different hypotheses entail different strategies. Sometimes the implications lead to similar activities for different reasons, and sometimes they suggest opposing strategies. For example, the recommendation to teach words for preexisting concepts is consistent with the strong cognition and local homologies accounts, but not necessarily with an interactionist explanation. Insofar as none of the available accounts are sufficiently powerful to predict what is necessary for a given child on a given linguistic task, the major implication is that the interventionist's responsibility is to choose activities with an awareness of the assumptions they entail. An understanding of why certain activities may or may not be successful will contribute to an appreciation of the nature of the child's problems, and to the development of guidelines for subsequent decisions.

In short, the cognition hypotheses have not fulfilled their early promise as explanation for children's early language acquisition. On the other hand, they have spawned a range of explanations that contribute helpful perspectives. We now extend those perspectives to new cognitive constructs, and to language learning beyond the early stages.

Chapter 4

Cognitive Implications of Communicative Competence

The competing accounts of the cognition/language relationship described in the preceding chapters share a common perspective, an emphasis on object-based knowing. The controversies concern what goes on in an individual child's mind as he explores the physical environment, the world of toys, food, vehicles, and other objects of importance to a child. Piaget's model of a child's mind focuses concern on the youngster's private mastery of objects and their actions and interrelationships. Within the Piagetian perspective, language acquisition is an individualized cognitive task, a matter of recognizing regularities in linguistic patterns that conform to conceptual units that have been worked out on a nonlinguistic basis. The child's task is to express what he knows, and what he knows is the world of objects.

The emphasis on objects is also evident in the dominant paradigms of American cognitive psychology. Experiments typically involve the manipulation, interpretation, or recall of collections of objects, usually colored geometric shapes. Many studies are inspired by an interest in the individual child's increase in knowledge and the principles that govern the restructuring of that knowledge, the ontogenetic perspective of Piaget.

The focus of children and objects has been a productive one. The extensive contemporary empirical literature and the richness of the debates attest to the value of the perspective. However, the dominance of the model contributes to a tendency among child language scholars to regard it as a complete characterization of the nonlinguistic underpinnings of children's linguistic knowledge and to define the cognition/language relationship entirely within the Piagetian viewpoint.

In this chapter we discuss aspects of children's linguistic competence and underlying cognition that are not included in the previously described models of cognition and language (Figure 2). Much of the preceding discussions of language dealt with the expression of propositional meanings, in words and word combinations. Here we expand our concern to rules for adjusting language to social context and to the linguistic context of extended discourse. Children's competence with these aspects of language implies three kinds of underlying knowledge not widely ascribed to children: person knowledge, social categories, and event knowledge.

Communicative Competence

So far our discussion of language has conformed to the assumptions of the traditional linguistic approach to the study of language. Among those assumptions are: the sentence is the highest level of analysis; speaker judgments of grammaticality are primary sources of evidence; linguistic rules are not influenced by context; and one function of language, that of assertion, is of primary significance. Obviously, these assumptions are not well suited to the study of early language acquisition, where sentence fragments are debatable, speaker judgments are unobtainable, contextual influence is apparent, and imperatives and interrogatives appear as well as assertions. The assumptions also are not helpful when one wishes to account for the way adults actually use language in their daily interactions with each other.

A group of language scholars who study language in its sociocultural context (Hymes, 1962, 1964; Labov, 1972; Schegloff, 1968; Sudnow, 1972) proposed a counter set of assumptions. They argued that linguistic rules are evident at the level of discourse; that some kinds of linguistic knowledge are only observable in context, when speakers behave according to rules they may not be aware of; that linguistic rules vary as a function of context; and that the functions of language are diverse and include imperatives as well as assertions. Hymes (1972) introduced the term *communicative competence* to refer to a speaker's knowledge of socially appropriate speech. The theoretical assumptions as well as the observational, descriptive methods associated with this model are appealing to investigators of child language who are trying to characterize the rules that govern children's verbal interactions in natural contexts.

By the late 1970s, *communicative competence* had become the umbrella model linking investigators with diverse interests in children's language (Ervin-Tripp & Mitchell-Kernan, 1977). Contrary to Piaget's characterization of early language as a child's attempt to express what he knows without regard to the perspective of his interlocutor, we now know that even young children master contextually based discourse rules. Children adjust their communication according to what they intend to accomplish, their available linguistic alternatives, and the social context, which includes such factors as the age and status of the person they address. Furthermore, youngsters' knowledge is systematic, comprehensive, and evident in a variety of circumstances.

A number of observations contribute to these conclusions. Preschool children use words like *can, will, he, it, this, that, a,* and *the* in a manner appropriate to the listener's perspective and information shared with the speaker (Macnamara, 1982; Maratsos, 1976, 1979b; Shields, 1978); they know styles of talk appropriate for different groups of people, such as babies, parents, and doctors (Anderson, 1977); they know how to adjust their own speech to suit their intent and listener, such as using hints or adding *please* when they want an adult to do something for them (Ervin-Tripp, 1977); they learn setting-specific communication codes, such as "school talk" (Dore, 1977); they can carry on a conversation (Keenan, 1974), describe everyday events (Nelson & Gruendel, 1979), and relate stories (Botvin & Sutton-Smith, 1977; Kemper, 1984; Watson-Gegeo & Boggs, 1977). During the school years, children gradually master the appropriate use of polite, direct, and explicit requests and directives (Ervin-Tripp, 1976; Garvey, 1975; Read & Cherry, 1978; Wilkinson, Calculator, & Dollaghan, 1982).

These competencies are of a different sort than the ones discussed in the preceding chapters that involve a match between words and referential meanings. Socially based adjustments and discourse skills are not amenable to explanation by underlying notions of object permanence or categories of objects, actions, or properties of objects. Instead, other kinds of knowledge are implicated. In order to adjust his communication to the perspective of a listener, a child must know something about the listener; in order to use linguistic forms that are appropriate for a member of a certain social group, the child must understand something about group membership; in order to tell a story, a youngster must be able to draw upon his knowledge of events.

Person Knowledge

A contemporary axiom of child development is that preschoolers are egocentric. This is attributed to Piaget, who observed that young children often seem to talk aloud to themselves, as if they do not intend nor expect a response from others (Piaget, 1955), and that youngsters are unable to determine the point of view of another person viewing a mountain (Piaget and Inhelder, 1969). The egocentrism is regarded as a consequence of cognitive limitations—an inability to consider one's own perspective simultaneously with that of another's. With further maturity, children gradually learn to decenter and consider more than one thing at a time.

This interpretation of youngsters' abilities is challenged by scholars who believe that even young children know about people as well as things, that people knowledge is fundamentally different from object knowledge, and that people knowledge is intimately linked with early communication skills (Bretherton, McNew, & Beeghly-Smith, 1981; Macnamara, 1982; Shields, 1978; Trevarthan and Hubley, 1978). They argue that in order to communicate a child must have mental representations for people that include how others represent the world (and the child) to themselves.

People knowledge is revealed in how children adjust their use of language to the social context, especially during the interpersonal exchanges in ongoing conversations. Shields (1978) unpacked the psychological awarenesses implicit in the superficially simple interchanges of nursery school children involved in play. She reasoned that the patterns of language use, such as modal auxiliaries (*shall, will, can*), deictic devices (*this, that, he, she, it*), and time reference (*now, then*) indicate children's representations of the perceptions, intentions, experience, and memory of others. Furthermore, this person knowledge is fundamental, "the underlying substratum of his (a child's) success in interacting with persons," and precedes more differentiated knowledge such as social roles (p. 552).

Shields hypothesized a number of constant features in a child's psychological model of a person. These features are said to "have begun to form as the child builds up communicative skill" (p. 553):

1. Persons have identity over time despite changes in location, behavior, and appearance.

2. Persons are self-moving or animate, and influence over the course of their behavior has to be negotiated by invoking interest or a shared frame of constraint.
3. Persons identify each other and can react to each other.
4. Persons can see, hear, touch, and smell, i.e., they have a perceptual field.
5. Persons intend their actions.
6. Persons conceptualize and construct their world in roughly similar ways.
7. Persons have moods and states such as anger and fear, and also wants, likes, and dislikes.
8. Persons can send and receive messages based on gestures and words that are related to context in stable ways.
9. Persons have an action potential, i.e., things they can and can't do.
10. Persons can retain previous experience and structure their present behavior by it.
11. Persons can replicate previous behaviors in new contexts.
12. Persons share sets of rules about what is appropriate within particular frames of action.

Shields' model is supported by Bretherton et al. (1981). They concluded that by 2 years of age children have an "explicit, verbally expressive theory of mind," evident most clearly in the ability of 20-month-old children to verbally represent internal states as experienced by themselves and others, e.g., *ouch/owie, sleepy, yucky, nice.* Their data supported each of Shields' 12 points and suggested two additional ones:

13. Interpersonal behavior is regulated by reciprocal consent using words such as *let, may,* and *may not.*
14. The internal states of others are not always unambiguously expressed and may have to be inferred from statements such as: "Is T mad at me?" "Moo. D'ya hear?"

The claim that young children know about persons as well as objects expands the possible nonlinguistic sources of language. However, the direction of influence is not clear. In the available studies, person knowledge is inferred from how children use language. In fact, that is Shields' (1978) major point: that by careful observation and logical consideration of how children use language, we can deduce their social awarenesses, and, ultimately, the "growth of man's concept of man" (p. 556). Yet one cannot infer the directionality of influence under such circumstances, nor did Shields explicitly attempt to do so. Bretherton et al (1981) assumed that the 12-feature person model proposed by Shields is a "minimum prerequisite for the occurrence of communication." This assumption, however, is premature. It is not yet clear whether this set of psychological awarenesses precedes and is necessary for language, or if it develops concurrently with language acquisition in some complex interactive network (as Shields implied) or if language itself serves to signal some aspects of person awarenesses that are not fully realized until the child learns linguistic codes or rules for use.

There are other cautions as well. The assertions that person knowledge is separate from object knowledge and is more fundamental are open to debate. Uzgiris (1981) argued against both premises. She proposed that the two kinds of knowing interact with and influence each other. Another caution concerns the evidence for the influence of person knowledge on linguistic competence. For example, although young children know that "persons intend their actions," they may not bring that knowledge to bear on linguistic distinctions, such as interpreting a parent's question "Is the door open?" as an intended demand to open the door. Instead, children rely on situational cues instead of speaker intent (Ervin-Tripp, 1978). Children may know about intentions in the basic sense of being able to take the view of the other. However, they can infer what the other has in mind regardless of the particular structure of the linguistic message.

These cautions notwithstanding, the study of communicative competence focuses on the idea that young children know about specifiable dimensions of their own and others' psychological functioning. Understanding the nature of children's person knowledge is essential to the acquisition of sociolinguistic rules. Whatever the nature of the interrelationship, it is difficult to account for how children manage to adjust their language to social contexts without some kind of person knowledge. Furthermore, it is possible that some of the children who are unable to master the subtle adjustments required in interpersonal communication lack basic components of person knowledge. Children who do not properly use *this* or *that*, or *can* or *will*, may lack not the relevant semantic contrasts but the sociolinguistic contrasts associated with their use. If such is the case, social factors may play a greater role in the difficulty than linguistic ones.

Social Categories

Children's awareness of social groups is revealed in how they talk. As Ervin-Tripp (1978, p. 246) put it, "When we address someone, or make a request, we do at least two things at once. We accomplish a communicative act such as calling out, or requesting, and we also convey our social categorizing of them and of our relationship."

Social categories determine the appropriateness of alternative ways of saying the same thing. If a child wishes to request a cookie, there are a variety of options available, such as *Give me a cookie, please; Cookie; Gimme that; I would like a cookie; Does this cookie belong to anyone?; My mother always lets me have a cookie after dinner;* and so on. The choice of options depends upon the addressee and the social context. Certain attributes of the addressee, such as age, sex, relative status, and familiarity, determine the degree of politeness and directness of request. These social categories are linked with rules governing the choice of linguistic alternatives for addressing and requesting, and other sociolinguistic phenomena as well, such as polite forms, code switching, rules for carrying on a conversation, and setting-specific communication rules (e.g., "school talk").

Preschool children adjust their comments to suit the listener and situation. They know that baby talk is appropriate for babies and animals; they know that they can be bossy to peers and subordinates but that polite forms are more appropriate for older children and adults unless they are trying to wheedle something from a peer; that social forms such as *Bless you* following a sneeze or cough are appropriate for humans but not animals; that different roles require different forms of address, such as *Doctor, Pastor, Mrs.,* or *Miss;* and so on.

The task is complicated by the fact that social categories overlap, e.g., sex and status (males as dominants), sex and roles (women as mothers), age and status (older children have greater status than younger children), and familiarity and roles (familiar parents, unfamiliar astronauts). Therefore, the relationship between social category and socially determined linguistic alternative rarely demonstrates a 1:1 correspondence, i.e., a single set of linguistic forms for a single social category. Sometimes selection of the appropriate alternative (for example, a polite form) will be overdetermined (a male teacher), whereas other times the rules associated with intersecting categories may compete with each other (if the teacher is a personal friend of the family, the child will have to choose between *Bob* and *Mr. Jones* as address forms).

Although it is widely accepted that youngsters distinguish between groups of people (such as familiar versus unfamiliar, or male versus female), these categories are not commonly linked with linguistic distinctions. Current conceptions of the cognitive substrata of language tend to overlook social categories, yet they seem to parallel object categories. The equivalence-determining principles of category formation apply to people, status, and role as well as objects. Social categories may be more abstract, insofar as they are inferred from subtle patterns of interactions and social behaviors. Some, such as sex and age, have physical correlates that can be readily discerned, but others, such as status and role, are not permanent qualities of the speakers. However, the same can be said of object-related categories such as possession and transient, graduated properties such as *hot*. Another parallel is the internal structure of social categories. For adults, social categories are internally organized around a prototypic member, in a manner much like object categories (Cantor & Mischel, 1979).

The linkage between sociolinguistic alternatives and underlying social categories allows for investigations of the hierarchies among groups and the boundaries separating groups. For example, if polite forms are determined by status, age, and sex, one could cross age and sex to determine their relative status, or one could vary the age and sex attributes to determine the category boundaries. This method of inferring social categories could contribute to contemporary efforts to determine the particulars of children's sex role knowledge (Huston, 1983) and the internal structure of social categories.

The inference of social categories from associated linguistic rules returns us to the measurement problems discussed earlier, and the possibility of circular reasoning about the direction of influence. That is, is evidence of social categories inferred from observations of language use, and in turn used to account for the acquisition of those sociolinguistic rules? There are nonlinguistic manifestations of social distinctions; for example, dominance is indicated by posture, eye contact, and physical distance. However, sociolinguists have emphasized the symbiotic nature of the language–social category relationship. Gumperz (1972, p. 15) argued that some social concepts such as status and role are manifest only in the system of linguistic alternations: "The division between linguistic and social categories is thus obliterated." This claim that linguistic and nonlinguistic knowledge are conflated is directly parallel to the strong cognition hypothesis. However, in this case the alleged direction of influence is reversed; the emphasis is on language as an explanation for cognition rather than vice versa. Ervin-Tripp (1977) observed that language may introduce social distinctions to a child, serving as an "instructional milieu for learners regarding the major social dimensions and categories of groups they join" (p. 152). Bowerman (1981) concluded: "to the extent that socially important concepts can be inferred *only* through communicative interactions, and have no direct nonlinguistic correlates, acquisition of them could not take place independently of language.''

The key to determining the direction of influence is the extent to which linguistically expressed social distinctions are not evident in nonlinguistic behaviors or cues, such as facial expressions, dress, and patterns of interpersonal interactions. The strategies for exploring the relationship between cognition and language that were reviewed earlier could be applied to this issue as well. For example, case studies of "natural experiments" would be helpful. One possibility is observation of children whose speech does not mark social category distinctions but who demonstrate sensitivity to social distinctions in other ways.

However, this approach is complicated by the fact that there are at least two reasons why children may not demonstrate sociolinguistic variations. One is that they may not understand the sociolinguistic rules. The other is that they may have a restricted set of linguistic alternatives as a consequence of grammatical limitations. For example, a child may rely on simple imperatives for requests (e.g., *Gimme that*) because he cannot manage the more complex grammatical structures of indirect requests (e.g., *I would like the cookie*).

Another special population of interest is the deaf. Without access to the social distinction conveyed by linguistic alternations, they may be less sensitive to social constructs. For example, Kusché and Greenberg (1983) reported that deaf children are delayed in their acquisition of the socially determined evaluative constructs of good and bad and that they have an early delay of role-taking ability that disappears by age 6. On the other hand, deaf children may learn to indicate social distinctions in their manual communication. Descriptions of socially determined variants of sign language could be compared to the sociolinguistic variations of the native verbal language. That comparison could then be related to observations of social behaviors of signing and speaking children.

Obviously, any understanding of children's social categories and the manner in which they are united with language is rudimentary. However, there is no doubt that the connection is there. Social categories are an important kind of nonlinguistic knowledge that children draw upon as they acquire communicative competence.

Event Knowledge

Much of the current debate about cognition and language has concerned the congruence between nonlinguistic and linguistic categories. Categorical knowledge is generally regarded as a relatively static organization of abstract bundles of things that are similar in some way. The categories that have received the most study are those that are organized in a hierarchical fashion, such as robin/ bird/animal. However, many of the regularities inherent in the world do not correspond to static categorical organization—for example, the established sequences of events involved in playing a game, relaying a message via the telephone, or preparing and eating a meal. Indeed, much of our real-world knowledge is organized in a sequential manner; the parts are connected on the basis of temporal and causal contiguities instead of static properties or attributes. These regularities are evident in ongoing activities that have a dynamic character, as opposed to the more stationary nature of categories. Such sequentially organized knowledge is referred to as "event knowledge." The notion has roots in schema theory, a holistic interpretation of how humans represent real-world knowledge. The idea of schema representation has a long tradition in social psychology.

More recently, schema theory has been influential in studies of memory (e.g., Mandler, 1979; Nelson, Fivush, Hudson, & Lucariello, Note 12) and artificial intelligence (e.g., Schank & Abelson, 1977). Essentially, a schema is a mental structure whose elements are related to one another on the basis of spatial, temporal, or causal contiguities instead of class membership and similarity relationships that are the framework of object categories. According to Mandler (1979), a schema "consists of a set of (usually unconscious) expectations about what things look like and/or the order in which they occur." Schemata can be general or specific, and can be formed "for anything with which one is familiar, from the details of appearance of a Hepplewhite chair, to the procedure required to cook a souffle, or the events that occur during a trip to the theater" (Mandler, 1979). Two kinds of schemata have been differentiated, those based on spatial organization (such as knowledge of the normal appearance of a kitchen), and those based on sequential organization (such as knowledge of how to obtain, consume, and pay for food in a restaurant). It is the latter that is of interest here.

The characterization of event knowledge is not definitive. For example, possible levels of abstraction and the nature of hierarchical structuring are commonly debated. The models that have been proposed (e.g., Schank & Abelson, 1977) are in the process of evolution (e.g., Abelson, 1981, Note 13; Schank, Note 14).

However event knowledge is to be depicted, it is clear that young children have acquired some sort of general understanding of familiar sequences of events. Nelson (1981) concluded that script knowledge in young children is general in form, temporally organized, consistent over time, and socially accurate. Her conclusions are based on a number of studies with children ranging in age from 3 to 8 years. The children were asked to tell "what happens when. . ." they engaged in familiar activities such as eating dinner or going grocery shopping. Even 3-year-olds were able to relate reasonably accurate sequences of events.

Another source of formal observation of children's sequential knowledge is their comprehension and production of stories. Elementary-age children rely heavily on familiar sequences for comprehension and recall of stories (Kemper, 1984; Mandler, 1978). Four-year-olds can detect inconsistencies and anomalies in script-based stories (Wimmer, 1979). The formal evidence is consistent with informal observations of preschool children at play, where they often act out long sequences of familiar activities, such as the preparation of meals, telephone conversations, and trips to the grocery store (e.g., Garvey, 1977). Schank and Abelson (1977, pp. 222–237) reported that children as young as 2 years indicated knowledge of routine events and suggested that certain sequences may be learned as early as 4 months of age.

Event knowledge is alleged to be primary in several senses: it is the infant's first means of organizing and representing reality; it is the basis of subsequent categorical representations; and it remains a primary means of mental organization for adults (Mandler, 1979; Nelson, 1981; Schank & Abelson, 1977). Nelson (1981) argued that awareness of social roles derives from a child's representation of familiar sequences. As children experience the same person in the same role in different sequences—for example, the teacher in a variety of school-day sequences—they are able to abstract the role category by generalizing similarities across contexts. According to Nelson, a child moves from a "rather direct representation of dynamically experienced relationships to an increasingly more general, abstract and therefore more static and categorical representation."

The recognition of children's event knowledge enhances our understanding of children's communicative competence. First, the notion of a sequentially based representation is an appropriate way to characterize the conceptual underpinnings of some of the linguistic phenomena of interest. Much of a child's communicative knowledge is inherently sequential in nature. For example, the rules for maintaining a conversation are based on the ability to deal with temporally contiguous speech events. Indeed, some conversational settings, such as the telephone, consist of well-defined familiar sequences, such as starting a conversation with *hello,* then determining the identity of the caller and the nature of the call, followed by a variable length of discourse in which turn-taking is closely maintained, and concluding by saying *good-bye.* The mental representation and memory mechanisms involved in such interactive communicative exchanges are surely sequential in nature.

Other linguistic phenomena are linked with event knowledge indirectly. For example, Ervin-Tripp (1978) reported that children draw heavily upon their practical reasoning and their understanding of common event sequences to infer the appropriate action response to an indirect request. If a parent with an arm full of grocery bags says "Is the door open?", a child would open the door regardless of whether or not he understood the question to be a request. Ervin-Tripp suggested that such redundancies in natural context contribute to a child's mastery of indirect requests.

Event sequences may serve as the basis for the development of categories. This possibility has several implications for how we interpret the linkage between cognition and language. In the previous discussion, children's use of sociolinguistic variants was linked with social categories, such as age, sex, and role. However, it may be that children first learn these variations in the context of familiar sequences of events—their everyday routines. This is analogous to the way that Piaget envisions object knowledge to be acquired in a child's actions with the objects. For example, polite requests may first apear at the dinner table. Children may then generalize to sequences sharing one or more features of the dinner routines, such as presence of an authority figure and use of polite terms. Such generalizations would become the equivalence structures of a categorical grouping (e.g., greater status/polite forms). If such is the case, the direction of influence between cognition and language may be more complex than current models suggest: from event sequences to patterns of language use and the concurrent mastery of routines of appropriate language to social categories. Linguistic conventions may serve as a vehicle for the child to move from one kind of nonlinguistic mental representation to another.

As in the cases of person knowledge and social categories, our understanding of the particulars of the relationship between event knowledge and linguistic rules is speculative. In particular, we need further support for the claim that event knowledge is primary and the closely related assertion that the sequential nature of event knowledge accounts for categorical learning. Although the nature of its influence is open to debate, it is hard to imagine how a youngster could manage to master rules for conversation without some dynamic representation of ongoing sequences.

Conclusions

Just as our model of the linguistic knowledge acquired by children has expanded to include social and discourse context, so must our conception of the associated conceptual knowledge. Recent demonstrations have revealed children's person knowledge, social categories, and event knowledge. This knowledge was not previously attributed to children. It enriches our conceptions of the nonlinguistic knowledge available for children to draw upon when learning language. Linguistic distinctions may both mark this knowledge and shape its development. Person knowledge, social categories, and event knowledge have emerged as strong candidates for functional linkage with language acquisition, although the specifics of the relationships have yet to be formulated.

Chapter 5

Acquiring the Logical Syntax of Language

Many fundamental aspects of language have not been acquired by 5-year-old children. Between the ages of approximately 5 and 14 years children master the use of relational terms, quantifiers, adjectives, adverbs, verb tense, aspect, mood, voice, and the ability to embed and coordinate clauses. Furthermore, during these years children acquire the matalinguistic knowledge necessary to judge synonymy and acceptability and to use figurative language.

Two competing theoretical accounts have been put forth for the gradual mastery of these aspects of linguistic competence. They share the assumption that knowledge constrains language development. They differ regarding the nature of the knowledge that is relevant to language acquisition. Stage-oriented cognitive theorists have stressed the importance of the growth of cognitive structures and operations for the development of language skills between 5 and 14 years of age. For example, the failure of a 6-year-old child to answer correctly the question *Is the doll easy to see?* when asked in reference to a blindfolded doll is attributed to a cognitive limitation on "decentration." The doll is judged hard to see because the child is unable to differentiate his own perspective from that of the doll.

In contrast, strategy-oriented theorists point to the difficulty of arbitrary and inconsistent morphological and syntactic constructions. Fragmentary and incomplete grammatical rules, supplemented by nonlinguistic strategies, are indicated by children's errors in comprehension and memory. However, strategy-oriented theorists disagree as to whether nonlinguistic perceptual and cognitive strategies or specifically linguistic principles and processing heuristics are used. In either case, internalization of the correct grammar is constrained by the processing strategies that the child uses. For example, the misinterpretation of "easy to see" constructions arises from the child's reliance on linguistic strategy. The child erroneously assumes that the noun phrase most closely preceding a verb is the subject of that verb. Although this assumption is generally true of English syntax, it is violated by the "easy to see" sentence. In these approaches, then, children's immature linguistic competence is attributed to incomplete or inaccurate knowledge.

Stages

Piaget's characterization of mature adult thought as governed by a lattice of logico-mathematical operations (Inhelder & Piaget, 1958, 1964; Piaget, 1970; Piaget & Inhelder, 1969) forms the cornerstone of the cognitive stage approach to syntactic development. In this view, language is structured by the child's thought in the same way that other symbolic systems, such as imitation, imagery, and play, reflect the child's cognitive structures and operations. As the child acts upon and transforms reality, a system of formal operations is gradually internalized. The formal operations, in older children and adults, form an axiomatic, logical calculus. This mental calculus corresponds to a Boolean algebra and defines a lattice of truth-functional, deductive propositional operations. A group of four functions governs these propositional operations: Identity (I), Negation (N), Reciprocity (R), and Correlative (C). The Negation and Reciprocity functions are reversible; they describe truth-functional ways of reversing the basic binary operations. For example, the negation of "p" (a proposition) is "not-p" and the negation of two conjoined propositions "p + q" is "not-p + not-q." The reciprocal of the disjunction of two propositions "p v q" is "not-p v not-q" and the reciprocal of "p + not-q" is "not-p + q." The Identity function leaves an operation unchanged so that the identify of "p" is "p." The Correlative function changes conjunction to disjunction; the correlative of "p + q" is "p v q."

This INRC group of functions defines the structure of mature thought. It is gradually mastered in three stages:

1. Piaget's stage of preoperational thought is characterized by the absence of these logico-mathematical functions. Consequently, children's thought is static, egocentric, and nonreversible. The preoperational child fails to appreciate class entailments and logical necessity. Relations between sets of objects

or actions and objects are ordinal, unidirectional, and unidimensional. For example, when asked to group together like objects, a preoperational child may form geometric shapes or patterns such as a square flanked by two triangles.

2. During the stage of concrete operations, children have acquired a semilattice that does not have the full deductive power of the INRC group. However, the semilattice does permit concrete operations such as class inclusion and complementation. The concrete operational child is capable of decentration and reversibility and capable of appreciating multidimensional and dynamic relations. A concrete operational child can form hierarchical classes that may be associated and negated. The child may sort geometric forms into piles of blue ones ("b") and not-blue ones ("not-b"). However, these operations can only be applied to objects actually present.

3. The attainment of formal operational thought expands the combinatorial power of the logical system to include disjunctive relations. Deductive reasoning about hypothetical relations and necessary and sufficient implications is possible. Thus, a formal operational child can reason about classes and logical relations in the abstract.

Reasoning about classes and logical relations between objects is but one area in which a logico-mathematical calculus governs thought. Inhelder and Piaget (1958) also examined how it determines children's approach to solving mechanical puzzles. A pendulum consists of a length of string and a suspended weight; the child's task is to discover what determines how rapidly the pendulum swings. The string may be long ("p") or short ("not-p"), the weight may be heavy, ("q") or light ("not-q"), and the pendulum may swing rapidly ("r") or slowly ("not-r"). Preoperational children lack the lattice of binary operations governing logical relations; their approach to the puzzle is haphazard. A preoperational child may compare a long and heavy pendulum ("p + q") and a short and light one ("not-p + not-q") and conclude that how rapidly she pushes the weight determines how rapidly the pendulum swings. A concrete operational child may draw upon the acquired partial lattice of logico-mathematical operations to investigate some logical combinations and to systematically observe their outcomes. Thus, the child, may observe that a long and heavy pendulum swings slowly ("p + q $\Rightarrow$ not-r") whereas a short and light one swings rapidly ("not-p + not-q $\Rightarrow$ r"). From these comparisons, the concrete operational child may correctly but not validly conclude that the length of the string, and not the weight, of the pendulum determines its frequency of oscillation. The formal operational child will recognize that all combinations of length and weight must be investigated. Only from systematically observing that a long and heavy pendulum swings slowly ("p + q ⇒ not-r"), that a long and light one swings rapidly ("not-p + q ⇒ r"), and that a short and light pendulum swings rapidly ("not-p + not-q ⇒ r") can the correct conclusion be validly reached.

This Piagetian characterization of the logico-mathematical foundations of thought has led to the investigation of the development of the logical syntax of language. Natural languages, like formal algebras, contain connectives, relations, quantifiers, and formal, structural operations. Consequently, the mastery of the logical syntax of language may be contingent upon the prior mastery of logico-mathematical structures and operations (Inhelder & Karmiloff-Smith, 1978; Sinclair, 1971, 1978). Two general patterns linking the development of syntactic abilities to the development of formal operations have been proposed:

1. As in the strong cognition model discussed earlier, the use and comprehension of particular syntactic or morphological devices may be linked to the attainment of specific stages of cognitive development. For example, the use of relational terms such as "smaller than" or "heavier than" may depend on attaining the stage of concrete operations as defined by performance of conservation tasks.
2. As in the local homology model, a related view is that certain formal cognitive operations may be prerequisite for specified linguistic operations. In particular, "reversibility" as a characteristic of concrete operational thought has been cited as a cognitive operation that is a direct precursor for the use and comprehension of comparative adjectives and passive voice.

Strategies

The gradual acquisition of complex linguistic devices may reflect the heuristic strategies the child uses to interpret and organize linguistic inputs and to deduce morphological and syntactic regularities. Strategy-oriented theorists point to the importance of cognitive processes that are independent of Piagetian stages of development. Two major types of processing strategies have been put forth: (1) "operating principles" and formal linguistic universals that limit the range of possible solutions to the mapping problem entertained by the child; and (2) perceptual and conceptual strategies that govern the interpretation and production of linguistic forms in the absence of complete grammatical analysis. These include probabilistic "guessing" strategies and perceptual segmentation heuristics as well as basic developmental processes such as rote recapitulation, analogical reasoning, and abstraction. As general cognitive processes, these strategies permit communication in lieu of complete mastery of grammatical rules and serve as "bootstraps" for the acquisition of morphology and syntax.

On the basis of cross-linguistic comparison, Slobin (1973) proposed a set of operating principles for the induction of language-specific grammatical rules. These operating principles implicitly rank linguistic devices in terms of their ease of acquisition. Those syntactic and morphological rules mastered early in the course of language development typically correspond to underlying conceptual distinctions that are conveyed by regular, discrete, and ordered postpositional morphemes. From this observation, Slobin proposed that children solve the mapping problem by relying on a set of innate predispositions that constrain the child's hypotheses about the form of language-specific syntactic devices. These operating principles include mandates to pay attention to the ends of words, to avoid exceptions, to avoid interruptions and rearrangements, and to expect that linguistic forms will be systematically patterned and that underlying semantic relationships will be overtly and clearly marked by patterned linguistic forms. Other, formal constraints on the mapping of underlying syntactic and semantic relations onto surface sentence forms have also been suggested (Wexler & Culicover, 1980). Such formal constraints serve to limit possible solutions to the mapping problem by limiting the types of syntactic rules and operations permitted by the grammar.

A parallel theoretical approach has been to propose other, nonlinguistic strategies that govern segmenting and organizing linguistic units. Unlike Slobin's operating principles, such nonlinguistic strategies are derived from more general perceptual and conceptual processes. Typically, the underlying nonlinguistic process is probabilistic: rather than relying on a fixed rule for the interpretation or production of a linguistic message, the child responds on the basis of a probability analysis. For example, Strohner and Nelson (1974) have argued that a "probable event" strategy is used by 2- and 3-year-olds to interpret active and passive sentences in lieu of the syntactic analysis of word order and sentence voice. As a result, these young children systematically misinterpret actives and passives that describe improbable events such as "The fence jumps over the cow." Over the course of language development, feedback regarding errors resulting from the use of probabilistic processes can provide information to the language learner about the correct mapping of semantic knowledge onto linguistic devices.

A third type of strategy is exemplified by the perceptual segmentation strategies of Bever (1970). These strategies are applicable to the analysis of linguistic stimuli as well as visual and auditory ones. As general principles, Bever's perceptual processing strategies govern the segmentation of ordered arrays on the basis of discontinuities, the avoidance of assigning multiple functions simultaneously to single stimuli, and the resistance of segments to interruption by other segments. Consequently, both mature language users and children learning language have difficulty establishing the correct segmentation of constructions with embedded relative clauses such as *The dog the cat was scratching was yelping*. One clause is embedded within another, there is no relative pronoun to mark the clause boundary, and the dog is simultaneously the subject of one verb and the object of another.

Finally, conceptual strategies based on general inductive heuristics for analyzing, organizing, and storing information can also lead to specific linguistic strategies when applied to the interpretation of linguistic inputs. MacWhinney (1978, 1982) has argued for the use of three such strategies: rote memorization of syntactic units, the formation of new syntactic patterns by analogy to old ones, and the creation of ordered combinations on the basis of individual stimuli, features abstracted from sets of stimuli, or category prototypes. Although these three strategies of rote, analogy, and combination are not specific to language, they are major strategies for the acquisition of morphology and syntax.

Probabilistic strategies, perceptual segmentation strategies, and conceptual analysis strategies, like Slobin's operating principles, govern the acquisition of particular morphological devices and the mastery of specific syntactic constructions. We next examine how children master relational terms, verb inflections and auxiliaries, and the embedding and coordination of clauses. In each case, the types of explanations, those couched in terms of Piagetian logico-mathematical functions and those based on perceptual and conceptual strategies, are considered. Then, we reconsider the roles of Slobin's operating principles, formal syntactic constraints, and inductive heuristics in the acquisition of syntax. Finally, we examine the development of metalinguistic abilities and the use of figurative language.

Relational Terms

For *more* or *less* to *in* and *on*, psychologists have focused on the comprehension and production of relational terms to demonstrate the dependency of grammar on stages of logico-mathematical thought or nonlinguistic strategies. Typically, experimental tests are used to evaluate children's knowledge of the meaning and use of morphological devices such as comparative and superlative suffixes (e.g., *big*, *bigger*, and *biggest*), spatial and temporal prepositions (e.g., *in*, *on*, *before*, and *after*), and quantity and mass terms (e.g., *some*, *all*, *more*, and *less*). Linkages between correct comprehension and production and Piagetian operational thought or errors arising from nonlinguistic strategies emerge as children act out test sentences with toys, select sets of objects in response to commands, or describe pictures and other objects. Stage-oriented theorists argue for links between logico-mathematical operations and the logical syntax of language by showing that children in the preoperational and concrete operational stages differ in their descriptions of object relations. In contrast, strategy-oriented theorists point to apparent shifts in the meanings of relational terms in different linguistic or extra-linguistic contexts as evidence for the use of nonlinguistic strategies in the absence of thorough mastery of the morphological devices. Strategies for responding with the simplest motor act, the most probable event, or the most preferred object can result in systematic misinterpretations or inconsistent patterns of interpretation when children have incorrectly or incompletely learned the relational term.

The importance of logico-mathematical operations for using relational terms was initially demonstrated by Sinclair-de Zwart's (1969) studies of preoperational and concrete operational children. Four- and 5-year-old children typically fail tests of their ability to recognize that quantities of water or clay or numbers of objects are not affected by distortions of visual appearance. Such tests of children's ability to conserve quantity, mass, or number across visual transformations distinguish Piaget's stage of preoperational thought from his stage of concrete operational thought. The emergence of a semilattice of reversible, but not disjunctive, logico-mathematical operations enables 6- and 7-year-old children to compensate for visual distortions and to conserve quantity, mass, and number.

Sinclair-de Zwart (1969) has observed that this shift from preoperational to concrete operational thinking is accompanied by a shift in how children describe arrays of objects. Preoperational children use absolute terms (e.g., *tall* for an object that is taller than the others), use similar terms for different dimensions (e.g., *small* for objects that are either short or thin), and restrict their descriptions to a single dimension (e.g., *big* for an object that is both tall and thin). Inhelder (1966) has further noted that the use of differentiated comparative terms and multidimensional descriptions is correlated with the ability to seriate objects differing in length. Lacking reversibility, preoperational children are unable to describe a stick they have described as *longer* than another as *shorter* than a third.

These observations about preoperational and concrete operational children's use of relational terms do not necessarily indicate a causal connection between logico-mathematical operations and the mastery of morphology. Although Sinclair-de Zwart has succeeded in teaching preoperational children to use different, comparative terms and multidimensional descriptions, such training does not directly lead to improvements in conservation or, hence, to operational thinking. Furthermore, performance differences between preoperational and concrete operational descriptions can be explained not by reference to a lack of reversibility, but by appeal to nonlinguistic strategies. The actual performance of preoperational children results from their incomplete analysis of the meaning of complex relational terms and their reliance on compensatory nonlinguistic strategies.

The role of nonlinguistic strategies in the comprehension of relational terms has been clearly demonstrated by Carey (1978). Following the pioneering work of Donaldson and Balfour (1968), children have been considered to pass through three stages in their use of *more* and *less* when they are asked to select the tree with *more apples* or to make a tree so that it has *less apples* on it. Initially, children treat *more* and *less* alike and respond nonsystematically or incorrectly to both; during an intermediate stage, children may respond correctly to the instructions with *more* but systematically err on *less*. Eventually, children come to respond correctly to both *more* and *less*. Carey's (1978) explanation for these three stages in the mastery of *more* and *less* is that children rely on a variety of nonlinguistic strategies in responding to instructions containing unfamiliar terms. One consequence of these strategies is that they may respond alike to polar opposites when they have not fully analyzed the meaning of one or both terms.

Carey asked 3- and 4-year-old children to adjust the quantity of water in a beaker so that it had *more* or *less* or *tiv* water in it. By comparing the children's responses to the nonsense syllable with their responses to *more* and *less*, she was able to document six major patterns of responding:

1. Some children failed to differentiate *tiv, more,* and *less*. They might add water, pour some out, or fail to respond to the three terms.
2. A second group of children responded as might adults. They added water to the beaker in response to *more*, poured out

some of the water in response to *less,* and questioned the meaning of *tiv.*

3. A few children demonstrated correct understanding of *more* but responded alike to *less* and *tiv.* Carey interpreted this pattern as indicating that the children recognized *tiv* as a nonsense syllable and treated *less* as another nonsense syllable. Consequently, they failed to respond or responded in some irrelevant way to *tiv* and *less.*

4. Some children clearly knew the meanings of both *more* and *less* yet did not treat *tiv* as a nonsense syllable. A preference for adding water to the beaker determined the children's response to *tiv.*

5. Carey was unable to interpret unambiguously the performance of children in the fifth group. These children initially questioned *tiv* but subsequently added water to the beaker for *more, less,* and a second occurrence of *tiv.* Carey suggested that these children, like those in group 3, knew the meaning of *more* and treated both *less* and *tiv* as nonsense syllables. Unlike the children in group 3, these children perseverated in adding water to the beaker.

6. Finally, Carey observed a single child who responded alike to *more* and *less* by adding water and questioning the meaning of *tiv.* For this child, apparently, *less* means *more.*

One implication of Carey's work is that preoperational children, who do not possess the logico-mathematical functions necessary to fully analyze relational terms, rely instead on nonlinguistic strategies including preferences and perseveration. This implication has been confirmed by more direct comparisons of the response strategies of conservers and nonconservers by Hudson, Guthrie, and Santilli (1982). Children were classified as conservers or nonconservers according to their performance on a number of conservation tasks. The correctness of their responses to questions requiring them to judge *more* and *less* and their explanations of their responses were linked to their cognitive level. Conservers made fewer errors on *less* and were more likely to offer explanations involving simultaneous comparisons of the objects than were the nonconservers.

Similar linkages between characteristics of Piagetian preoperational thought and the reliance on nonlinguistic strategies has been proposed in the domains of temporal relations (e.g., *before* and *after*), spatial relations (e.g., *in, on* and *under*), and deitic terms (e.g., *here* and *there,* or *this* and *that*) (Beilin, 1975; Cromer, 1974, 1976; Ferreiro & Sinclair, 1971; Webb & Abrahamson, 1976).

Verb Inflections and Auxiliaries

Verb inflections and auxiliaries typically indicate four types of information about an event: whether it occurred before the present time (tense), the manner, duration, habitualness, or repetition of the event (aspect), the speaker's attitude toward the event's occurrence (mood), and the syntactic role of the event's agent (voice). For example, in English the regular -ed marks past tense, the progressive -ing and the perfective has mark aspect, and the modal auxiliaries, e.g., may, can, and should, mark mood. Not surprisingly, both Piagetian logico-mathematical operations and nonlinguistic strategies have been linked to children's correct production and comprehension of verb tense, aspect, mood, and voice. Children must not only master the appropriate linguistic devices to mark these properties of events, but must also be able to represent past events, contrast static, progressive, or punctual events, judge possibility, necessity, permissiveness, and obligation, and determine agency and passivity.

However, apart from studies of the mastery of active and passive syntactic constructions, little research has documented the role of cognitive operations in the mastery of verb auxiliaries and inflections. Some research simply traces the emergence of these linguistic devices or probes for children's comprehension of contrasts in tense, aspect, or mood (Fletcher, 1979; Hirst & Weil, 1982; Kuczaj & Maratsos, 1975; Limber, 1973). Other research on these linguistic devices has focused on children's tendency to overgeneralize morphological devices for marking verb inflections to static verbs, producing seed, feeled, or haved. They may treat noncausative verbs as causatives, as in I'm gonna fall this on him or Come her! Such errors appear to have a predominately linguistic basis deriving from children's difficulty in classifying the verbs as transitives or intransitives or in learning linguistic-specific constraints on word formation. Two observations suggest that it is unlikely that such errors depend on cognitive misunderstandings of action-state distinctions or cause-effect relations: first, errors such as He is knowing her or other stative verb plus progressive inflections do not occur (Maratsos, Kuczaj, Fox, & Chalkley, 1979) and, second, children do not produce novel causative verbs until relatively late, after they have used causatives correctly (Bowerman, 1974).

Some studies of the acquisition of verb tense, mood, aspect, and voice suggest a weak link between children's abilities to decentrate and conserve and the use of verb auxiliaries and inflections. Cromer (1968, 1974) analyzed the longitudinal development of tense and mood markers in the spontaneous speech of two children. Initially, the children's utterances preserved the temporal order of the events described. Gradually, the children came to describe events reversed in temporal order and to pose hypothetical events. In each case, the children adopted a previously available linguistic device as a vehicle for the expression of the newly emerging contrast in tense or mood. Eventually, they acquired the syntactic competence to use verb auxiliaries and inflections to indicate tense and mood. Slobin (1966) has noted that the emergence of grammatical mood in Russian is delayed relative to the expression of hypothetical events by children. This observation, like Cromer's, suggests that attaining operational thought, including decentration, is a critical prerequisite for the mastery of verb tense and mood.

Stronger evidence for the linkage of Piagetian operational thought with the mastery of auxiliary verbs and inflections was obtained by Beilen (1975). Children were tested on reversibility tasks involving ordering a series of pictures denoting time-dependent events, e.g., the growth of a tree. Their success or failure on the reversibility tasks was compared to their performance on tests of their understanding of past, future, progressive, perfective, and conditional auxiliaries and inflections. As measured by the incidence of correct answers to questions constructed around the target linguistic devices, language performance lagged behind the attainment of reversibility. Operational thought appears to be a prerequisite for the use and comprehension of the past progressive -*ing* as in *The car was winning,* the perfect auxiliary *has* in *The car has won,* and the conditional auxiliary *will* in *The car will win.*

The acquisition of sentence voice also appears to be contingent on operational thinking. Most studies of children's understandings of sentence voice require them to act out test sentences with toy figures. Sinclair and Ferreiro (1971) compared children's performance on acting out active and passive sentences to their own descriptions of similar events. A link between the use of linguistic devices for marking voice and cognitive operations was apparent. Comprehension of the active and passive sentences gradually improved with the children's ability to describe both the agent and patient of the action and to execute both the syntactic reordering and verb modifications necessary to produce passives. Sinclair and Ferreiro suggested that the operations of decentration and reversibility are essential prerequisites for the full mastery of voice.

Beilin (1975) has confirmed a link between the comprehension and production of passive sentences and operational reversibility. Poor performance on comprehension tests and the inability to produce well-formed passives was coupled with poor performance on tests of operational reversibility. French and English bilingual children who have mastered operational thinking show a similar improvement on tests of sentence voice in either language (Tremaine, 1975). Although operational reversibility does not guarantee correct comprehension and use of sentence voice, it does appear to be a cognitive prerequisite for correct performance with actives and passives.

As in the case of relational terms, children who have not yet fully mastered the use of tense, aspect, mood, and voice rely on a variety of perceptual and cognitive strategies for comprehending sentences with auxiliary verbs and inflections (Bever, 1970; Cromer, 1971; Strohner & Nelson, 1974; Turner & Rommetveit, 1967; Weil & Stenning, 1978). For example, 5-year-old children may correctly act out passive sentences that involve nonreversible actions such as *The cup is washed by the girl.* The use of a strategy that takes the first noun phrase in a sentence to be the agent of the action will lead to correct performance on active sentences and systematically incorrect performance on passives. Yet other strategies may rely on perceptual and contextual factors such as object saliency, spatial location, and discourse cues for the interpretation of auxiliaries and inflections. Gradually, as children master the syntax of verb tense, mood, aspect, and voice, their dependence on such strategies fades.

Syntactic Connectives

Natural languages, like formal logics, include a variety of connectives to describe conjunction, disjunction, and implicature relations among sentence constituents. Sentence constituents may be connected by *and, or, but, both/and, neither/nor, either/or, if/then,* and *if and only if/then.* Subordinating connectives state temporal and causal connections such as *because, since, although, unless, despite, before, after, when, while,* and *until.* Negation may be used in combination with these connectives to expand the possible relations. Natural languages also include a variety of devices for embedding clauses, such as relative clauses and noun and verb phrase complements.

The full adult repertoire of linguistic connectives and sentence structures has barely begun to emerge by age 4. The children studied by Bloom, Lahey, Hood, Lifter, and Fiess (1980) acquired, in order of emergence, *and, and then, when, because, what, so, then, if, but,* and *that* by 36 months. They used these connectives to express additive, temporal, causal, and adversative relations as well as to mark relative clauses. However, the full range of syntactic forms had not yet been mastered. Complex syntactic constructions including noun and verb phrase complements and subordinate clause constructions are mastered gradually throughout the school years (Chomsky, 1970; Flores d'Arcais, 1978; Goodluck, 1981; Ingram, 1975; Limber, 1973). For example, 5-year-olds do not correctly interpret *Daisy hits Pluto after putting on the watch* and prefer an incorrect interpretation in which Pluto puts on the watch. Even 10-year-olds are likely to err in interpreting the propositional truth and entailments of sentences such as *This is a monkey unless it has a trunk.*

Tremaine (1975) has clearly demonstrated that children learning a second language show significant increases in their comprehension of syntactic relations when they attain concrete operations. Operational bilingual French- and English-speaking children performed better than preoperational children on tests of their understanding of relative clauses and possessive complements as well as other syntactic structures such as direct and indirect objects and reflexive pronouns. Operational thinking was a significant factor in predicting performance on either French or English constructions even when age, grade level, and curriculum were controlled.

Comprehension of the phrasal connectives *and, not,* and *or* is also linked to level of performance on Piagetian tests of operational thinking. Beilin (1975) has correlated children's performance on nonlinguistic classification tasks with their accuracy in following instructions such as *Give me the dolls that are not girls* or *Give me the dolls that are not boys.* Achievement of operational levels of performance on the nonlinguistic tasks preceded comprehension of the parallel linguistic connectives. Furthermore, operational thinkers showed superior performance on all connectives relative to the performance of preoperational thinkers. Complete comprehension of all tested linguistic connectives had not yet been attained by 8- and 10-year-olds who had partially achieved formal operational thinking. Thus, the development of a complete lattice of logical functions appears to be a prerequisite for the use and comprehension of complex syntactic structures and linguistic connectives.

Natural language inferences have proved to be non–truth-functional in that reasoning with natural language does not conform to the formal rules of propositional or syllogistic logics (Wason & Johnson-Laird, 1972). One consequence is that natural language connectives cannot be directly mapped only to truth-functional connectives of propositional logic. For example, it is difficult to arrive at the correct, "logical" conclusion that "If George does not stay sober, then he gets depressed" from the two premises "George does not stay sober only if he doesn't keep on his diet" and "Either George keeps on his diet or else he gets depressed." Practical inferential reasoning strategies based on plausible causal relations interfere with deriving the logical inference. Other biasing strategies include predilections for conjunctive rather than disjunctive relations, for weighting positive information more than negative information, and for treating temporal juxtapositions as causal connections. The truth-functionalness of children's inferences gradually improves, although adults are still prone to non–truth-functional inferences (Paris, 1975; Wason & Johnson-Laird, 1972).

Competing Accounts

The research reviewed above is consistent with weak linkages between the acquisition of the logical syntax of language and the development of cognitive operationality and the concomitant functions of reversibility and decentration. Furthermore, this research suggests that preoperational children, but not operational children, use a variety of cognitive strategies to interpret relational terms, verb inflections and auxiliaries, and sentential connectives. However, this account of the acquisition of the logical syntax of language is not without its critics; two competing accounts have been put forth. Both decouple the acquisition of syntax from the acquisition of Piagetian operational thought, and both minimize the role of cognition-based strategies such as the probable-event strategy or the minimum distance principle. By one account, general inductive procedures have been proposed as heuristics for the construction of grammatical rules. Syntactic categories and rules are determined on the basis of distributional regularities in the use of syntactic reorderings and grammatical morphemes. Inductive heuristics guide this learning process (Kuczaj, 1982b; Mac-Whinney, 1978, 1982; Maratsos, 1979b; Maratsos & Chalkley, 1980; Maratsos & Kuczaj, 1978). In contrast, linguistic universals and predispositions are invoked as constraints on the learning of syntactic rules. These constraints may be quite general "operating principles" (Slobin, 1973, 1979) for constructing grammatical rules or quite specific principles for relating the underlying and surface structures of utterances (Wexler & Culicover, 1980). In either case, constraining principles that are themselves not part of the grammar of a particular language delimit the range of possible rules for any particular language. The postulation of either specific linguistic constraints or general inductive heuristics is an alternative to linking syntactic acquisition to the development of cognitive operations.

Inductive Heuristics

Many contemporary scholars, echoing earlier approaches to the acquisition of morphology and syntax, argue that the analysis of distributional regularities in the child's linguistic environment by general inductive heuristics is sufficient for the acquisition of syntax (Kuczaj, 1982b; MacWhinney, 1978, 1982; Maratsos & Chalkley, 1980). This approach to the acquisition of surface structure relations and form classes assumes that the acquisition of grammar is independent of cognitive development. Furthermore, processing strategies are not merely nonlinguistic ways of interpreting unfamiliar linguistic constructions, but, rather, are active procedures for acquiring the correct syntactic rules. Thus, the child may assume that syntactic rules are governed not by abstract structural notions but by semantic and distributional regularities.

One implication of this approach is that the application of grammatical rules may, initially, be limited to only a part of the adult range. Such a situation may arise when the child has based the use of a grammatical rule on an incorrect or misleading analysis of the prevailing semantic or distributional regularities. For example, the passive construction in English is not restricted to any particular class of semantically defined verbs. Passives may involve actions, states, and relations. Maratsos, et al. (1979) have shown that children's mastery of the passive may not extend across this entire range, but rather may be limited to specific verbs or verb classes. Thus, a child might correctly interpret *Goofy was washed by Donald* but err with *Goofy was liked by Donald*. Actional and non-actional verbs are apparently assigned to different form classes and the passive rule is initially applied only to the class of actional verbs.

This disassociation of syntactically similar linguistic devices is also noted in children's acquisition of the auxiliary system. Maratsos and Kuczaj (1976; 1978) and Maratsos et al. (1979) argued that the auxiliary verbs are not acquired as a homogeneous system. Rather, the sequence of omitted auxiliary–misplaced auxiliary–correctly placed auxiliary is repeated anew for each auxiliary verb and each syntactic construction. For one child they observed, the modals *can* and *could* were correctly used in declarative sentences while only *can* appeared in yes/no questions. Kuczaj and Maratsos argued that the low incidence of auxiliaries coupled with their heterogeneous semantic and distributional regularities is responsible for the lack of generality in their acquisition. Consequently, it is difficult to determine the correct form classes and syntactic rules governing the English auxiliary system.

MacWhinney (1978, 1982) has described three basic processes by which children may learn word-order regularities: rote, analogy, and combination. Rote memorization appears to be responsible for children's production of interrogative forms that combine *why not* with a sentential or verb phrase, e.g., *Why not cracker can't talk?* and the creation of redundant strings such as *That's makes a truck* or *It miss it cowboy boot.* Novel syntactic patterns may also be produced by analogy to old ones. Thus a child may say *The Daddy is at work* with reference to her own father in analogy to such forms as *the dolly* and *the book*.

Rote memorization and analogy are not sufficient explanations for the acquisition of grammatical regularities. Consequently, MacWhinney has described four general heuristics for producing novel combinations: predispositions, bound rules, free rules, and class-bound rules. The ordering of noun phrases or other sentence constituents within a clause may be determined by certain cognitive predispositions. Thus, the most informative or the most complex element may occur initially. Agency, salience, and perspective may also determine word or phrase order regularities. Clause order, in turn, may be governed by predispositions to order causes before results or to order a temporal reference point after an asserted event. Bound, free, and class-bound rules apply to sets of lexical items, sets defined by abstracted semantic features, or sets defined by semantic features as well as distributional regularities, respectively. For example, MacWhinney (1975) argued that 42 bound rules generated 85% to 100% of the 11,077 utterances of two Hungarian children he studied. An English example is the production of interrogative phrases by binding a wh- word to individual lexical items, e.g., *Where Mommy?* and *Where pencil?* Syntactic rules may be governed by abstracted semantic features common to a set of lexical items. For example, the agent-action order of children's early utterances arises from such a free rule. Agency, potency, mobility, causality, and perspective may define the range of children's productive and interpretive syntactic rules. Finally, syntactic rules may be bound to semantically and paradigmatically defined classes. For example, the state-process distinction must be supplemented with a distributional analysis to separate adjectives and verbs. Both the semantic features and distributional regularities are required to block the production of such forms as *He fonds the dog* (Maratsos & Chalkey, 1980).

The use of rote and analogy and the induction of item-bound, free, and class-bound rules have been traditional approaches to the analysis of child language acquisition. Compare MacWhinney's use of rote, analogy, and combination to similar heuristics proposed by, for example, Braine (1963, 1976), Hull (1943), and Staats (1968). These approaches have in common the assumption that a grammar is composed of form classes. Such taxonomic approaches to the acquisition of syntax are subject to a number of criticisms (See Bever, Fodor, & Weskel, 1965a, 1965b; Fodor, Bever, & Garrett, 1974; Steinberg, 1982). Such critics argue that semantic and distributional analyses are insufficient for the induction of syntactic rules and for explaining observed patterns of language acquisition. Chief among these objections is the claim that inductive heuristics and semantic and distributional analyses cannot block the production of ungrammatical utterances. As an alternative, other scholars of child language acquisition have proposed innate linguistic universals and formal syntactic constraints.

Linguistic Constraints

Based on cross-linguistic data from children acquiring over 40 different languages, Slobin (1973, 1979) has suggested that linguistic universals guide the segmentation of linguistic inputs into grammatical elements and the formulation of grammatical rules. These universals are based on a set of initial expectations, or "operating principles," for the structure of language. These operating principles include mandates to pay attention to the ends of words and the order of linguistic elements, to avoid exceptions to syntactic rules, and to assume that relations between words will be encoded by linguistic elements, that semantic relations will be overtly and clearly marked, and that the use of grammatical markers will make good semantic sense. These operating principles, in turn, generate a set of universal principles of language acquisition. These universals predict that: (1) postposed grammatical morphemes will be acquired earlier than preposed ones; (2) syntactic forms that violate word order regularities will be acquired later than those that do not; (3) linguistic markers will be acquired in the following order— no markings, appropriate markings in specific cases, overgeneralization of markings, and the full adult system of markings; (4)

grammatical systems that closely adhere to a one-to-one mapping between semantic relations and linguistic markers will be acquired earlier than systems that do not; (5) when the selection of linguistic markers is determined by arbitrary formal criteria, children initially will use a single marker in all contexts; and (6) semantically consistent grammatical systems will be acquired without error.

Other specific linguistic constraints on the acquisition of syntactic rules have also been proposed. These constraints are designed to permit the mapping of deep and surface linguistic structures by limiting the class of possible syntactic rules. The general argument is that the formal properties of language can be learned only if the child's generalizations from the linguistic input are so constrained. Wexler and Culicover (1980) have developed two such formal constraints: the freezing and the binary principles.

The freezing principle states that a grammatical transformation may not apply to any transformationally derived structure that cannot be generated by the base phrase-structure rules. For example, a dative transformation derives sentence 2 from sentence 1:

1. John gave a bone to his dog. [NP1 [V NP2 [Prep NP3]]]
2. John gave his dog a bone. [NP1 [[V NP3] NP2]]

The grammatical structure [[V NP3] NP2] of sentence 2 cannot be generated in the base. Consequently, the freezing principle prevents transformations from fronting or topicalizing NP3, but such transformations can apply to NP2. As a result, sentences 3a, 4a, and 5a are acceptable whereas sentences 3b, 4b, and 5b are ungrammatical:

3a. What did John give his dog?
 b. *Who did John give the bone?
4a. A bone, John gave his dog.
 b. *His dog, John gave the bone.
5a. A bone is tough for John to give his dog.
 b. *His dog is tough for John to give a bone.

The binary principle blocks the application of grammatical transformations across more than one clause boundary. For example, a grammatical tranformation may shift a noun phrase around the verb phrase of the main clause, as in 6b. The binary principle blocks the extrapolation of a noun phrase or prepositional phrase from within a clause and thus blocks sentences 6c and 6d:

6a. That John gave a bone to his dog impressed me.
 b. It impressed me that John gave his dog a bone.

c. *That John gave to his dog impressed me a bone.
d. *That John gave a bone impressed me to his dog.

Other such constraints on transformations include: the raising, no bottom context, and transparency constraints (Wexler & Culicover, 1980); the complement-command constraint (Goodluck, 1981); the conjoined-clause analysis (Tavakolian, 1981); and the backward anaphor restriction (Solan, 1981). These constraints both affect how children interpret transformationally complex sentences and enable them to learn the correct syntactic rules. For example, Goodluck (1981) has examined how 4- and 5-year-olds analyze participial and verb phrase complements. The complement command (or c-command) constraint blocks interpreting the object of a preposition as the missing subject of a participial complement, as in sentence 7a, or of an infinitive complement, as in 7b:

7a. Jim ran from the police after grabbing the jewels.
b. Jim was ordered by the thief to grab the jewels.

Although children typically follow a minimum distance principle and assume that the noun phrase most closely preceding a verb is its subject (Chomsky, 1970), this assumption is blocked by the c-command constraint. Consequently, as Goodluck has observed, children will typically err in interpreting Pluto as the subject of the complement in 8a but not in 8b:

8a. Daisy hits Pluto after putting on the watch.
b. Daisy stands near Pluto after putting on the watch.

Thus, the c-command constraint overrides the minimum distance principle for 8a; the c-command constraint does not apply to 8b and children rely on the minimum distance principle to interpret Pluto as the subject of the complement in both 8a and 8b.

This approach to syntactic acquisition, in contrast to Slobin's (1973), is contingent on a particular approach to the characterization of syntactic rules, namely generative transformational grammar. However, like Slobin's operating principles, the freezing, binary c-command, and other principles describe universal limits on the kinds of syntactic rules children formulate in the course of language acquisition. These operating principles and formal constraints are assumed to be innate and language-specific heuristics for formulating hypotheses about syntactic structures and rules. As such, they provide explanations for the acquisition of syntax that are not dependent on Piagetian cognitive development or on the use of heuristics for the induction of surface structure relations and form classes.

Metalinguistic Abilities

Language development is not limited to the mastery of phonological, morphological, semantic, and syntactic rules. Adults, but not young children, can not only produce active and passive sentences, but they can appreciate the near synonymy of pairs such as *The cow kissed the horse* and *The horse was kissed by the cow*. We adults recognize the ungrammaticality of *What we should do now?*, the anomaly of *Golf plays my sister,* and the non-literalness of *He's pushing up daisies*. Cazden (1972, 1975) and Gleitman, Gleitman, and Shipley (1972) have suggested that the acquistion of syntactic abilities is accompanied by the development of reflective metalinguistic abilities responsible for linguistic intuitions of acceptability, grammaticality, ambiguity, and synonymy. Even quite young children can judge the acceptability of sentences, although their judgments may be at odds with those of adults. The development of metalinguistic abilities has been linked to both the development of basic syntactic competencies and the development of concrete and formal operational thinking.

Quite young children are able to make metalinguistic judgments about the truth or falsity of affirmative and negative sentences. Pea (1982) has demonstrated that 2- and 3-year-olds can deny false affirmative sentences, e.g., *This is a car* in reference to a toy ball, and false negatives, e.g., *This is not a car* in reference to a toy car. The complexity of the linguistic devices children use to deny false sentences gradually increased with age. The youngest children used solitary *no,* whereas older children used negatives along with the incorrect object names or produced elaborate denials as well as corrections. Pea also noted that 2- and 3-year-olds can intentionally produce false identifications. For example, one child said *It's a battery. Oh, it's a biscuit* while looking at a biscuit and laughing.

Following the work of Gleitman et al. and of de Villiers and de Villiers (1972), most researchers have assumed that children's comprehension and production of a given syntactic device is a prerequisite for intuitions about the acceptability, synonymy, or ambiguity of that device. Thus, for example, de Villiers and de Villiers (1972) found that children who did not yet use word order in production or comprehension tasks did not reject as ungrammatical sentences with word-order violations. The development of the ability to judge sentence grammaticality shows an orderly progression (Gleitman et al., 1972). The judgments by young children are based on the content of the test sentence and, hence, implausible or unappealing sentences may be rejected (Carr, 1979; Gleitman et al., 1972). Older children appreciate semantic anomalies involving violations of selectional restrictions but not syntactic violations. Thus a 5-year-old may accept *John and Jim is a brother* but reject *I think that any rain will fall today* because he is less sensitive to violations of subtle syntactic rules than to semantic distortions (Bohannon, 1975, 1976; Gleitman et al., 1972; Howe & Hillman, 1973; James & Miller, 1973; Scholl & Ryan, 1975). Seven- and 8-year-olds are capable of judging syntactic deviance, as in *Boy is at the door* and *I saw the queen and you saw one* (Gleitman et al., 1972). Older children are able to learn to judge synonomy of meaning despite surface differences (Beilin, 1975; Sack & Beilin, Note 15).

Consonant with these gains in linguistic intuitions, children also evidence considerable improvement in their ability to use figurative language, including jokes and riddles (Fowles & Glanz, 1977; Hirsh-Pasek, Gleitman, & Gleitman, 1978; McGhee, 1974; Shultz, 1976; Shultz & Horibe, 1974) and metaphors (Billow, 1975; Gardner, Kircher, Winner, & Perkins, 1975; Gardner, Winner, Bechhofer, & Wolf, 1978). For example, Hirsh-Pasek et al. (1978) have examined children's ability to explain jokes involving different sorts of linguistic ambiguities. The fewest errors were made in explaining the jokes with semantic ambiguities of underlying structure or lexical items, e.g., *How can hunters in the woods find their lost dogs? By putting their ears to a tree and listening to the bark.* Jokes with syntactic and phonological ambiguities (e.g., *Where would you go to see a man-eating shark? A seafood restaurant*) were somewhat more difficult to explain. And the most difficult jokes were those involving an ambiguity of a morphological boundary, e.g., *How do trains hear? With their engine ears.*

On the other hand, the development of metalinguistic abilities must involve more than simply the mastery of the relevant syntactic and semantic rules. It appears that one or more aspects of cognitive development enter into the development of metalinguistic abilities. Links between Piagetian cognitive operations and children's use of metaphor and their judgments of synonymy, acceptability, and phonemic segments have been noted. For example, Arlin (Note 16) found that children categorized as preoperational on various Piagetian tasks could use representation metaphors (e.g., *My shadow is stretched*), that concrete operational children could, as well, use similarity metaphors (e.g., *My shadow is like a piece of the night*), and that formal operational children had, additionally, mastered proportional metaphors (e.g., *One lonely chunk of the night grows legs and follows me to school*). This finding that the type of metaphors children produce and understand is linked to preoperational, concrete operational, and formal operational ways of thinking is quite general (See Billow, 1975; Cometa & Eson, 1978).

The linkage of metalinguistic abilities to level of cognitive development has been carefully documented by Hakes (1980). He compared the nature of preoperational and concrete operational children's judgments of sentence synonymy and acceptability and their ability to segment words into phonemic units. Performance on the three metalinguistic tasks was significantly intercorrelated, indicating that all three share a common, underlying ability. This common metalinguistic ability gradually develops between 4- and 8 years of age. Furthermore, performance on the three metalinguistic tasks correlated with level of operational thinking as measured by several conservation tasks. Hakes suggested that a common cognitive ability is responsible for both metalinguistic judgments and operational conservation. Thus, the functional operations of reversibility and decentration are implicated in the ability to judge that *Teacher coughed the car* is "silly," to realize that *There is more cake than ice cream* means the same thing as *There is less ice cream than cake*, and to determine that *boot* has three phonemic segments.

However, more general cognitive abilities are also required to perform metalinguistic tasks. Keil (1979) has examined the role of formal constraints on ontological knowledge in a variety of metalinguistic tasks. He solicited judgments of sentence anomaly (e.g., *The cow was an hour long*), non-natural classes (e.g., the class of machines, events, and sentences), the acceptability of copredication (e.g., that something cannot be both ungrammatical and waterproof), and judgments of class similarity (e.g., that humans are more similar to plants than to liquids). Keil proposed that the ontological knowledge underlying these judgments is hierarchically organized and constrained to form a "non-converging" tree structure (the M-constraint). A similarly constrained hierarchial tree of predication corresponds to the ontological tree. For example, "a" and "b" of Figure 4 are partial ontological and predicability trees, respectively.

Four consequences follow from the constraint that the ontological and predicability trees are "non-converging". Sentence anomalies arise whenever a predicate is combined with a term from another branch of the tree, as in *a cow happened yesterday*. Non-natural classes occur whenever there is no node in the tree that dominates all and only the terms of the class, as in the class of cows and stories. Copredication is blocked whenever there is no "straight-line" path through the tree linking the predicates, so that something cannot be both red and true. Finally, class similar-

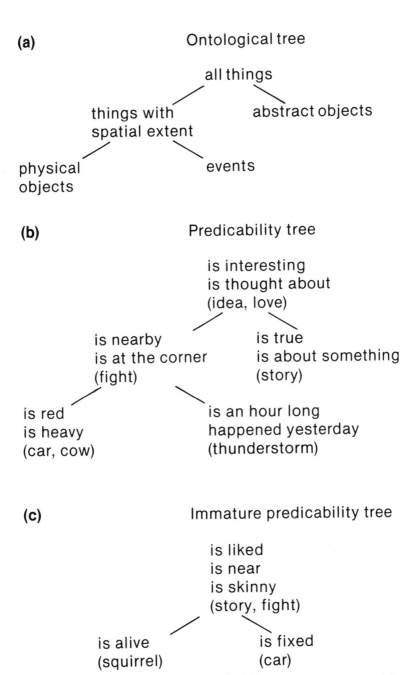

(a) Ontological tree

all things

things with spatial extent

abstract objects

physical objects

events

(b) Predicability tree

is interesting
is thought about
(idea, love)

is nearby
is at the corner
(fight)

is true
is about something
(story)

is red
is heavy
(car, cow)

is an hour long
happened yesterday
(thunderstorm)

(c) Immature predicability tree

is liked
is near
is skinny
(story, fight)

is alive
(squirrel)

is fixed
(car)

Figure 4 Keil's ontological and predicability trees governing metalinguistic judgments.

ity can be determined by the proximity of the classes in terms of the number of linking branches and nodes.

Although the judgments of both children and adults conform to the constraint prohibiting converging branches in the predicability tree, their ontological and predicability trees differ. For example, a kindergartner may only distinguish living things and functional artifacts from all other things, yielding a predicability tree like that in "c" of Figure 4. Such a child would judge that stories, as well as the pages making up the storybook, can be skinny, and that fights can be heavy. However, the child would agree that stories cannot be fixed and that cars are not alive.

Keil's work demonstrates that there is increasing differentiation of ontological categories: the most primitive ontological trees he obtained distinguished only between living things and all other things. Next, functional artifacts were differentiated from other things, then events, and finally abstract objects, were recognized as distinct ontological categories. The hierarchical organization of ontological knowledge thus determines the nature of children's metalinguistic judgments.

Conclusions

There appear to be three determinates of the acquisition of syntax by children between the ages of 5 and 14 years. As depicted in Figure 5, cognitive operationality (particularly the functions of reversibility and decentration), strategies for the induction of syntactic rules and for the interpretation of unfamiliar syntactic constructions, and universal linguistic principles and formal constraints interact to influence acquisition, use, and metalinguistic judgments of syntactic devices. The importance of cognitive operations, cognitive strategies and heuristics, and linguistic principles and constraints is clearly evident in research on the acquisition and use of morphology and syntax by language-disordered, cognitively impaired, and autistic children.

One account attributes problems of language acquisition to underlying conceptual difficulties, a position we discussed in Chapter 2 as part of the local homologies hypothesis. Recall that the argument runs like this: language-disordered children have language competencies comparable to younger normal children; they also perform below age expectations on some tasks of mental representation. Just as cognitive and linguistic performance parallel each other in normal development, so is it the case in delayed

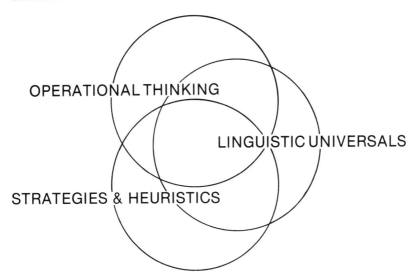

Figure 5 Determinants of the acquisition of syntax by children ages 5 to 14.

acquisition of language. Therefore, the cognitive deficiency contributes to the linguistic one (Leonard, 1979).

Embedded in this account is the characterization of the language of language-disordered children as like that of younger normal children. This conclusion, one that is dominant in the contemporary literature, is based on studies reporting that:

1. The syntactic complexity of language-disordered children's spontaneous utterances resembles that of younger, normal children matched for mean length of utterance (Morehead & Ingram, 1973).
2. Language-disordered children's acquisition of grammatical morphemes, including verb auxiliaries and inflections and comparative and superlative adjective inflections, follows the same order as that of normal children, although they use these morphemes less frequently (Ingram, 1975; Johnston & Schery, 1976; Kessler, 1975).
3. Language-disordered children do use complex syntactic forms, relational terms, and verb auxiliaries, although they do so less frequently and less consistently in their spontaneous speech than do age-matched normal peers (Leonard, 1972; Menyuk, 1964).

In short, children with language disorders do not demonstrate bizarre linguistic forms or rules that are unlike the language of normal children. Given the nonexistence of deviant linguistic acquisition, their linguistic competence is widely regarded as "delayed," that is, like that of younger normal children. The conclusion is challenged by recent work of Johnston and Kamhi (Note 11). Their comparison of language-disordered and normal children is at a more detailed level of analysis than was used in earlier studies. They compared the relationship between propositional content and syntactic structures in two groups of children matched for mean length of utterance—one group (age 4;6 to 6;2) diagnosed as language disordered and one group (age 3;8 to 4;1) with normal abilities. They reported differences between the two groups. Despite similar utterance length, the language-impaired children expressed fewer propositions per utterance and made more morphological and inflectional errors than the younger normal group. Johnston and Kamhi interpreted the findings as indicating asynchronous development across linguistic domains for the language-impaired group. In a similar comparison of mentally retarded children, normals, and language-disordered children all matched for mental age, the language-disordered children demonstrated asynchronies, unlike the other two groups (Kamhi & Johnston, 1982).

We conclude that the general parameters of language acquisition and syntax, in particular, are shared by normal, mentally retarded, and language-disordered children. On the other hand, some of the more subtle aspects of morphology manipulation appear to be suspect in the case of language-disordered children. To the extent that these children are not just "delayed" in their language acquisition, the logic of the mental-representation-deficit-as-causal argument is weakened.

It is also weakened by unexplained discrepancies in the comparison of cognitive performance across groups matched for age or linguistic abilities, as discussed in Chapter 2. For chronologically matched children, language-disordered children perform like their normal peers on nonverbal tests such as the Leiter. On a few tests, such as haptic recognition (Kamhi, 1981) and rotations of a visual array (Johnston & Weismer, 1983), language-disordered children are either less accurate or require more time than their normal peers. Yet sometimes these children perform better on cognitive tasks than do their language-matched but chronologically younger peers. In short, the cognitive competencies of language-disordered children are more like than unlike their comparison groups, and sometimes exceed their language matches.

All in all, the pattern of evidence is more consistent with language-specific processes than more general cognitive ones. The similarities between normal and language disordered correspond to the idea of robust universal linguistic competencies, especially if it can be demonstrated that these similarities conform to the structural principles and formal constraints of Slobin (1973) and Wexler and Culicover (1980). The subtle difficulties with morphological manipulations suggest problems with language-specific inductive strategies.

Another way of testing the relative contribution of cognitive and linguistic factors is to identify children who have a particular uneven profile of development: syntactic acquisition coexisting with cognitive deficits. Such is the strategy of Curtiss (1982) and her colleagues (Curtiss et al., Note 7). They have described three children (ages 6, 9, and 16) with apparently intact syntactic competencies yet with gross impairments of intellectual ability, as well as other unusual aspects of development. These children performed very poorly on tests of classification, operational conservation, and figure copying, drawing, and construction. Yet the children, including one with Turner's syndrome, were able to produce complex, well-formed sentences, such as *How am I ever gonna learn if I don't wash the car windows?* despite marked deficits in cognitive ability. The three children used passive, comparative, and wh- constructions as well as nominal and verb inflections. Curtiss et al. suggested that this dissociation of cognitive and syntactic abilities is evidence for the independence and autonomy of cognition and the syntactic aspects of language.

Such uneven profiles certainly are dissonant with the claim that linguistic and nonlinguistic competencies are components of a larger interrelated whole. These youngsters demonstrated syntactic abilities beyond rote, arbitrary aspects of syntax. Their syntactic forms expressed meaningful relationships between sentence constituents and between surface form and underlying syntactic structure. The three children produced well-formed utterances using a wide range of syntactic devices. However, it is difficult to characterize the nature of their syntactic knowledge. Curtiss acknowledged that the children were not consistent in their application of grammatical rules, and some morphological devices were used infrequently. In this respect, they are similar to language-disordered children. Curtiss and her colleagues emphasized the highest levels of grammatical performance. It is also possible that the factors contributing to the inconsistent or restricted application of grammatical rules are associated with the cognitive limitations. It may be that deficits in cognitive operations can lower the frequency, consistency, or pervasiveness of the use of complex syntactic forms, relational terms, and verb auxiliaries. In such cases, pockets of grammatical competencies emerge with no integrated syntactic competency. The individual and isolated competencies may be fragile and vulnerable to competing factors, such as fatigue or linguistic context. Such individual competencies may emerge as a consequence of partially independent inductive strategies of operating principles.

One other group of atypical children is of interest insofar as their performance suggests a causal role for cognitive strategies and heuristics. Autistic children typically exhibit delayed language—that is, language comparable to younger normal peers—in addition to aberrant social/emotional responses. Tager-Flusberg (1981) reported that autistic children have major deficits in their use of nonlinguistic strategies. Recall that normal children who have not yet mastered passive voice will use strategies based on word order and probable events to interpret passives. Like normal children matched for verbal and nonverbal abilities, the autistic children Tager-Flusberg studied were able to use a word order strategy: however, unlike the normal children, the autistic children did not use a probable event strategy. Tager-Flusberg suggested that the autistic children did not use semantic knowledge in interpreting language and thus had deficits in their analysis of form classes and semantic regularities.

Methodological differences in the studies of atypical children may contribute to conflicting findings regarding the role of cognitive impairments. Johnston, Leonard, and Tager-Flusberg have used comparative studies of the cognitive and linguistic abilities of normal and language-disordered children to argue that deficits in nonlinguistic representational abilities are causally linked in the acquisition and use of syntactic and morphological devices. In sharp contrast, Curtiss and her colleagues have employed extensive studies of the cognitive and linguistic abilities of individual children to argue for the autonomy of cognitive and syntactic abilities. For example (Curtiss et al., Note 7), Anthony at age 6 scored substantially below age norms on tests of visual embedding, hierarchical construction, copying and drawing, spatial concepts, classification, conservation, and logical sequencing. However, his auditory, verbal short-term memory performance was above age level. On tests of language comprehension, Anthony performed poorly in the areas of relational terms and inflectional morphology. However, his comprehension of active word order, wh- questions, and relative clauses was exceptionally high. In spontaneous speech he used a wide range of syntactic structures, although his use of inflections was problematic. Given this uneven profile, Curtiss concluded that Anthony's syntactic competencies are independent of his cognitive abilities in that he is able to comprehend and produce complex syntactic structures.

Similar methodological differences are apparent in, on the

one hand, the work of Beilen, which compares the performance of groups of preoperational and operational children on tests of active and passive sentences, and, on the other hand, that of Maratsos and Kuczaj, which carefully examines individual patterns in the emergence and use of morphological devices and syntactic structures. Comparative studies tend to suggest the hypothesis that language development is contingent upon characteristic ways of thinking or stages of cognitive development. Individual case studies generally reveal a heterogeneity of language development, suggesting that such development is dependent on general inductive strategies or language-specific constraints. A related methodological factor evident in studies of the normal acquisition of grammar is the difficulties inherent in studying the interaction of operational thinking, cognitive heuristics and strategies, and formal linguistic principles and constraints. Contemporary research has, almost exclusively, focused on a single morphological device or syntactic form and examined the contribution of one of these contributing factors. However, when one compares findings regarding a particular syntactic rule, the general, interactive nature of these contributing factors is apparent. For example, consider the acquisition of the active-passive voicing contrast. Beilen (1975) has shown that operational reversibility is a logical prerequisite for the production of passive sentences. However, as argued by Maratsos et al. (1979), passive voice is not acquired as a unitary syntactic device; rather, children must gradually work out the extent of this device across different classes of semantically defined verbs. Finally, the late acquisition of the passive voice is consistent with Slobin's (1977) claim that sentences deviating from the standard word order will be acquired late.

Given the influence of three factors for grammatical acquisition, any one of them, or a combination of several, could be at work in the case of an individual child who is having difficulty learning syntactic rules. The child who cannot transform an active sentence into a passive one, or who misinterprets the passive as an active construction, may do so because he lacks the notion of reversibility, or because his understanding is limited to a few verb forms, or because he is operating with a rigid application of a word order principle, or because he cannot interrelate the various factors in an appropriate manner. The nature of the difficulty would have a bearing on the selection of training strategies. The child who does not comprehend the principle of reversibility is not likely to benefit from instruction designed to teach privileges of occurrence for specific word classes in different grammatical slots.

Chapter 6

Consequences of Language

A paradox of the contemporary study of language and cognition is that mastery of language is believed to have both positive and negative consequences for cognitive functioning. On the one hand, many researchers, following Vygotsky (1962, 1978), assume that speech and language can facilitate action, perceptual discrimination, and memory. These beneficial consequences of speech and language result from the use of semantic categories to direct behavior and to control thought. However, others, following Whorf (1956), assume that language can interfere with memory and distort perception and cognition. The semantic and syntactic categories of one's native language may impose rigid limits on thought and action and, hence, have negative consequences.

Cognition Facilitated by Language

The 1962 English publication of Vygotsky's *Thought and Language* anchors one major approach to the study of linguistic influences on cognitive development. Written in 1934, this book, together with his essays (Vygotsky, 1978) from that same period, lays out a framework for the study of internalized, private speech and its role in directing cognition. Vygotsky described three periods in the development of speech:

1. At first, speech serves an interpersonal or parasocial function. It is used to communicate the speaker's intentions to others in order to solve practical problems.
2. Gradually, speech comes to accompany action and acquires an intrapersonal function of self-communication. Vygotsky argued that "the most significant moment in the course of intellectual development . . . occurs when speech and practical activity, two previously completely independent lines of development, converge" (1978, p. 25).
3. Eventually, speech comes to precede and determine action; speech thus becomes a means to guide and direct action. As speech acquires this planning function, it "turns inward" to become an internalized, "private" system. Speech becomes increasingly shortened and abbreviated and takes on a covert, subjective form. Vygotsky pointed to three uses of internalized speech: it directs and regulates action, it influences perception, and it facilitates memory.

Vygotsky sought to trace the development of speech from its initial interpersonal use to its eventual intrapersonal use. He studied the amount of overt, self-directing speech that children between 2 and 4 years of age produced across different tasks. The incidence of self-guiding speech increased across this age range as the children acquired the intrapersonal uses of speech to direct their own actions. Vygotsky presumed that the incidence of overt, self-guiding speech was curvilinear with age, first increasing from 2 to 4 years, then decreasing as speech was internalized. Vygotsky also demonstrated that the incidence of self-guiding speech varied with task difficulty and with the presence of auditors. More difficult tasks were accompanied by more self-guiding speech. When the children's activities were audited by strangers or deaf individuals or were accompanied by a loud band, the children produced less self-guiding speech than when other children like themselves were present. Vygotsky argued that the incomplete differentiation of self-guiding speech from true, social, interpersonal speech was responsible for this finding.

More recently, the development and use of private, self-guiding speech has been detailed by Kohlberg, Yaeger, and Hjertholm (1968). They offered a modification of Vygotsky's development sequence that includes five stages or levels:

1. Overt, private speech is initially the repetition of words, phrases, or sounds for the sake of play.

2. Overt, private speech is next used to "direct the behavior of nonhuman objects," e.g., *Let go, sticky tape*, and to describe one's own behavior. Such self-directed remarks are not relevant to solving the task at hand and serve no planning function.
3. Overt, private speech then becomes task relevant and self-guiding. It precedes and directs action and is used to answer the child's own questions about the task.
4. As speech becomes internalized, inaudible mutterings occur.
5. True, silent, inner speech is used to direct action.

Kohlberg et al.'s observations of children between 4 and 10 years of age supported this developmental hierarchy. Inaudible mutterings increased with age, becoming the dominant form of private speech for the 8- and 9-year-olds. The development of overt self-guiding speech was curvilinear, peaking at age 6. Self-descriptive speech steadily declined across this age range, and word play was relatively rare. Furthermore, the incidence and level of private speech positively varied with task difficulty. Finally, the incidence of private speech was curvilinear with respect to the mental age of the children. Intelligent 4-year-olds used more private speech than did average 4-year-olds, whereas average older children (6 to 10 years) used more private speech than did intelligent older children. Kohlberg et al. concluded that more intelligent children use self-guiding speech chronologically earlier than do average children, but that they also develop true, silent private speech earlier.

Wertsch has extended the Western view of Vygotsky's work by stressing the role of social interaction in the ontogenesis of cognition (Wertsch, 1979, 1983). Speech, because it is a sequential, analytic generalization and categorization of experience, transforms perception and action and is responsible for the reorganization of psychological processes such as attention, memory, and concept formation through social interactions. Wertsch has examined the transition from interpersonal to intrapersonal processes via speech during mother-child problem-solving interactions. Initially, social interaction is limited by the children's failure to grasp the integrity of the problem to be solved; consequently, mothers are unable to verbally regulate the children's actions because the children do not relate their mothers' directives to the task at hand. At the next level, the problem-solving situation is understood by the children but their understanding is limited to concrete, obvious aspects of the situation. Indirect or nonexplicit maternal directives are not obeyed because the children are unable to infer the necessary links between the mothers' indirect questions or hints and possible actions relevant to solving the problem. These inferences are made at the third level, although children are unable to develop a strategic plan for solving the problem. Finally, at the fourth level in the transformation of other- to self-regulation, children become able to solve the problem without verbal direction from their mothers' speech.

The mothers' directives are essential in the development of strategic self-regulation. First, the children must be verbally led to define the situation as a coherent problem, then they must be verbally led to infer the necessary connections between their actions and solutions to subparts of the problem, and finally they must be verbally led to devise overall strategies for solving problems. The importance of speech in this transition to self-regulation is seen as the mothers initially used directives that the children did not understand and then carefully guided the children in executing the actions necessary to carry out these directives. Such other-regulation of problem-solving actions is variant across situations (Wertsch, Minick, & Arns, in press) and its success may be limited by the linguistic or cognitive abilities of the children (Stone & Wertsch, Note 17).

Contemporary research on the study of facilitative effects of speech and language on cognition has focused on three questions: How does speech come to guide, direct, and control thought and action? How does speech come to mediate perceptual discriminations and choice behavior? And how does speech come to be used as an aid to memory?

Regulatory Role of Speech

Luria (1961) surveyed Soviet research that was conducted between 1945 and 1958 on the genesis of mental processes and voluntary action. As a result of this survey, he offered a refinement of Vygotsky's three periods or stages in the development of voluntary thought and actions. According to Luria: (1) initially, the external speech of adults is capable of initiating thoughts and actions— however, such external speech cannot inhibit actions; (2) gradually, external speech, of oneself or of others, acquires an inhibitory function and can suppress or limit motor responses and, hence, regulate behavior; and (3) finally, internalized speech comes to control thought and action. Luria's own research focused on the development of vocal and linguistic control over gross voluntary actions such as performing simple motor responses. Subsequently, a similar developmental sequence has been observed in the areas of perceptual discrimination, concept formation, and mnemonic processes of encoding and retrieval. Each of these areas, in its current formulation, shares with Luria's voluntary action hypothesis the assumptions that language and speech positively influence thought and action and that this determining influence gradually develops during the course of language acquisition.

Luria's (1961) demonstrations of the ontogenesis of the regulatory role of speech were deceptively simple. Children from approximately 18 months to $5\frac{1}{2}$ years of age were asked to execute a series of simple actions. By varying the complexity of the task and the nature of any concomitant vocal expression, Luria sought to trace the development of how internalized speech comes to regulate voluntary behavior. Like Vygotsky, Luria explicitly assumed that thought was equivalent to internalized speech and was therefore verbal, propositional, and linguistic in form and function.

Many of the studies Luria surveyed required children to press a rubber balloon in syncronicity with flashing lights and, on some occasions, a verbal expression such as *Go!* He was concerned with two distinct aspects of the role of speech in the regulation of such actions. The controlling function of speech shifts from an external focus to an internal one. At the same time, control shifts from the plosive, neurodynamic, temporal patterns of speech to its analytic, semantic content and syntactic form.

Evidence for these two increasingly regulatory functions of speech emerge across three stages:

1. Verbal instructions did not inhibit the motor responses of the youngest children of 18 months. Once they began to squeeze the balloon, these children were not able to synchronize their squeezing motions to instructions like *Squeeze* or *Don't squeeze* or *Squeeze when the light comes on*. Thus, only the plosive or impulsive aspect of external speech can influence behavior and only by initiating action.

2. As speech comes to have an inhibitory function, children between 3 and 5 years of age are able to respond correctly to instructions such as *When you see the light, squeeze the balloon*. However, perseverative responses may occur that can be suppressed when the motor task is accompanied with a verbalized *Go*. Instructions such as *When the light appears, press twice* may lead to many successive balloon pressings: the appropriate double squeeze can be produced when the motor task is combined with a double vocal response such as *Go, go*. Thus, the plosive, impulsive, rhythmic, neurodynamic aspects of external speech continue to regulate behavior, but speech is now able to both initiate and inhibit action.

3. By the age of 5 or 6, children succeeded in following complex instructions like *Don't squeeze when there is no light* without the necessity for external, vocal speech. Therefore, Luria concluded, the semantic content of internalized speech is regulating voluntary behavior.

The details of the experimental methods and procedures that Luria and his colleagues used are unknown, and attempts to replicate these studies have proved to be notoriously unsuccessful (Bronckart, 1973; Jarvis, 1968; Joynt & Cambourne, 1968; Meacham, 1978; Miller, Shelton, & Flavell, 1970). In particular, these researchers have failed to confirm (1) that, for some group of intermediate-age children, responses accompanied by speech are more accurate than those performed in silence, and (2) that the plosive, rhythmic aspects of speech initially exert control over motor responding in the absence of any semantic or syntactic analysis of the speech.

However, other researchers have reexamined Luria's hypothesis in light of the failure to replicate his findings. Wozniak (1972) argued that Luria used tasks in which the verbal response simultaneously accompanied the motor act and criticized the attempted replications for failing to observe this condition. To test this refinement of Luria's hypothesis, Tinsley and Waters (1982) compared the performance of 2-year-olds on a pegboard hammering task. The children either performed silently or while verbalizing. In one verbalizing condition, a semantically relevant verbal response (e.g., saying *one*) accompanied the action. In the second verbalization condition, a semantically irrelevant verbal response (e.g., saying *toy*) was used. In the third verbalization condition, the relevant verbal response preceded the action (e.g., the child said *one* and then hit the peg). When either verbal response simultaneously accompanied the action, the children's performance was facilitated in comparison to their performance in the silent condition. Relevant verbal responses that preceded the actions had a significant inhibitory effect. These results, then, clearly substantiate Luria's hypothesis: during this early period of language acquisition, overt speech does facilitate action and it is the plosive or impulsive aspect of speech that has this effect.

Despite limited contemporary support for Luria's account of the development of the regulatory role of speech, it has continued to be influential. Its influence derives in part from the intuitive appeal of this theory and in part because it is parallel to theories of the development of perceptual discrimination, concept formation, and mnemonic processes.

Mediational Role of Speech

In 1946, Kuenne (1946) proposed an account of perceptual discrimination by young children that stressed the importance of verbal mediation of perception. Kuenne trained preschoolers and kindergartners to consistently choose the smaller of two geometric figures. Once they had learned this response, the children were tested on a new pair of figures that differed in size from the training pair. Of interest was whether or not the children were able to transpose their response to the new figures and whether or not they verbally expressed the principle *Choose the smaller.* Kuenne noted two distinct patterns. The youngest children either failed to talk about the size of the stimuli or did so without linking size to their choice response, and were unable to transpose the correct solution to the new test stimuli. In contrast, the older children spontaneously mentioned the correct principle during the test or in response to questioning after the test, and were able to transpose this principle to the new test stimuli.

Kendler and Kendler (1959) found further support for the role of verbal responses in mediating perceptual discriminations and choice responses. They contrasted two different situations. In each, children initially were trained to, for example, select a square figure rather than a triangle while ignoring the color of the geometric forms. The children were then tested on how rapidly they could learn one of two new choice responses. In the reversal shift condition, the color of the forms continued to be irrelevant to the choice. However, the correct selection was reversed so that, for example, triangles were now to be chosen over squares. In the nonreversal shift condition, color became relevant to the choice and geometric form became irrelevant. Now, for example, green figures were to be selected over red ones. Evidence for the mediating role of verbal responses is based on three findings: (1) young children, e.g., kindergartners, have equal difficulty with reversal and nonreversal shifts; (2) however, older children learn reversal shifts more rapidly and accurately than nonreversal shifts; and (3) when young children are required to explain their choices, they are more likely to excel on the reversal shifts relative to the nonreversal shifts than are children who are not required to verbalize.

Verbal mediation is assumed to be responsible for the superior performance of older children on reversal rather than nonreversal shifts. For the older children, verbal mediators such as *Choose the square* are available and these mediators control their behavior. When confronted with the reversal shift, the children are able to modify the mediators into new appropriate ones such as *Don't choose the square*. For the nonreversal shifts, the children cannot easily modify the original mediators and, hence, must learn a new mediator such as *Choose the green one*. Requiring children to explain verbally their selections not only facilitates the acquisition of the appropriate mediators but also strengthens the control of the mediators over behavior.

The verbal mediation hypothesis (Kendler, 1972, 1979; Reese, 1962) suggests three stages in the development of verbal control of perceptual discrimination:

1. Initially, verbal mediators are not available; hence, the child's choice behavior is controlled by sensory and perceptual aspects of the environment rather than verbal responses or semantic distinctions. A production deficit thus limits the child's behavior.
2. Gradually, the child acquires verbal mediators; however, these mediators may not reliably control the child's choice behavior. Consequently, a control deficit limits the child's behavior.
3. Eventually, the verbal mediators reliably and consistently control the child's behavior. Choice responses are determined by verbal responses or semantic categories. Hence, neither production nor control deficits occur.

This verbal mediation hypothesis has not been without its critics. For example, Zeamon and House (1963) argued that the observed deficits in performance are due not to deficiencies in the production and control of verbal mediators, but to the failure of young children to attend to the relevant dimensions of the stimuli. Tighe and Tighe (1972) argued that a failure of discrimination, not attention, was responsible for the poor performance of young children. However, further support for both production and control deficits does come from studies of verbal mnemonic processes.

Mnemonic Role of Language

When adults are asked to remember a series of pictures or objects, they will typically verbally label the pictures, rehearse these labels, organize the labels into semantic or taxonomic categories, and use this organized verbal information to facilitate recalling or recognizing the pictures. A primacy effect is typically observed such that the first few items in the series are recalled more accurately than those from intermediate serial positions. Although the first few items in a series are likely to be rehearsed more than the remaining items, other verbal encoding and elaboration processes, made possible by the prolonged rehearsal, are apparently responsible for their recall advantage. Across several series, proactive interference, built up by these verbal mnemonic processes, can impair recall of taxonomically similar items; release from proactive interference occurs when recall is shifted to a novel taxonomically defined series. As a consequence of the verbal encoding processes, lists of semantically related items are recalled more accurately than series of unrelated items and semantic clustering will be typically observed as items from similar categories are recalled together. Finally, category labels, provided as cues, can prompt recall of specific instances that are organized in terms of these categories. See Atkinson and Shiffrin (1968), Kintsch (1970), Mandler (1968), and Shiffrin (1970) for reviews of this literature and specific models of adult memory.

Verbal mnemonic processes are concerned with three different phases of learning and remembering. These mnemonic processes include: (1) those that operate at the time of encoding, such as labeling, rehearsal, and elaboration; (2) those that involve the storage and organization of the information, including interference and categorization; and (3) those that occur primarily during retrieval of the information, such as category cuing. Marked developmental trends have been observed in those verbal mnemonics concerned with the encoding and retrieval of information. In contrast, those verbal mnemonics involved in memory storage and organization, such as categorization, appear to be developmentally invarient.

Encoding: When children between the ages of approximately 2 years and 5 years are asked to recall series of pictures or words, no primacy effect is observed (Atkinson, Hansen, & Bernbach, 1964; Hagen & Kingsley, 1968; Perlmutter & Meyers, 1979). Such young children do not spontaneously rehearse words or verbal labels for pictures, and verbal labels have little effect on young children's recall (Furth & Milgram, 1973; Kobasigawa & Middleton, 1972; Moely, Olson, Halwes, & Flavell, 1969). However, induced rehearsal can facilitate recall (Flavell, Beach, & Chinsky, 1966; Kingsley & Hagen, 1969). Furthermore, older chidren (e.g., sixth graders) employ more active rehearsal strategies, such as rehearsing sets of items rather than individual items, than do younger children (Ornstein & Naus, 1978). Young children do not verbally label pictures, and induced labeling has no effect on recall by 4- and 5-year-olds, can facilitate recall by 7-, 8-, and 9-year-olds, and can impair recall by 10-year-olds (Hagen & Kingsley, 1968; Kenney, Cannizzo, & Flavell, 1967).

Storage and organization: Proactive interference and release from proactive interference are observed in children as young as 3 years (Kail, 1976). Categorical clustering is observed in 2-year-olds' recall, and they will recall clusterable series better than nonclusterable ones (Perlmutter & Meyers, 1979; Rossi & Wittrock, 1971; Vaughan, 1968). Nonetheless, these developmentally invariant semantic and taxonomic effects are contingent upon the level of children's semantic knowledge and, hence, may be limited to particular types of words or relations at different ages or stages of semantic development (Lange, 1973, 1978; Rossi & Wittrock, 1971).

Retrieval: Kindergarten and first-grade children do not spontaneously use categorical information to actively guide their retrieval of information (Moely et al., 1969; Neimark, Slotnick, & Ulrich, 1971). Unlike 11-year olds, 7- and 9-year-old children do not spontaneously use a category-by-category retrieval strategy, although when prompted they can follow it (Salatas & Flavell, 1976; Scribner & Cole, 1972). From 6 to 11 years, children also get better at using recall cues given them (Kobasigawa, 1974). Thus, although they may have organized the information categorically, children under approximately 10 years of age do not spontaneously exploit this category information to devise efficient and exhaustive retrieval plans (Lange, 1978).

Normal children between the ages of approximately 5 and 10 years thus appear to suffer from deficits in their production of verbal mnemonic strategies to encode and retrieve information (Flavell, 1970). They do not spontaneously rehearse labels or use category information to direct memory search. However, when prompted to do so, these children are able to improve their recall through the use of these strategies. Thus, control or mediating (Flavell, 1970) deficits are not observed. It is not clear whether even younger children consistently have control deficits such that they are unable to use verbal mnemonics when prompted to do so. In the case of verbal labeling, prompted use of this strategy does not lead to improvements in the recall performance of 4-year-olds (Hagen & Kingsley, 1968; Kenney et al., 1967). However, Myers and Perlmutter (1978) have demonstrated some effects of categorical and semantic knowledge on 2- to 4-year-olds' recall and recognition. They suggested that verbal mnemonics, when employed, have automatic facilitative effects.

Mentally retarded children have deficits in their strategic use of verbal mnemonics to encode, store, and retrieve information. In studies of retarded adolescents, typically no overt rehearsal is observed and there is no primacy effect across serial positions (Belmont & Butterfield, 1969; Brown, Campione, Bray, & Wilcox, 1973;

Ellis, 1970). Retarded individuals' use of category retrieval strategies is poor and the advantages of categorizable series over non-categorizable series are reduced (Goulet, 1968; Jenson & Frederiksen, 1973). Training retarded individuals in the use of rehearsal, categorization, and other verbal mnemonics is successful and can lead to long-term improvements in their recall performance (Kellas, Ashcraft, & Johnson, 1973; Nye, McMannis, & Haugen, 1972; Ross, Ross, & Downing, 1973).

Discussion

The following effects of acquiring a native language on cognition are facilitative: control of speech and language and regulation of behavior, provision of verbal mediators for perceptual discrimination, and guidance of the encoding, storage, and retrieval of information. However, one hypothesis about the relation of language and thought does not seem to be supported: Luria suggested that, during an intermediary stage of development, overt speech, but not internalized speech, can regulate behavior. Although overt verbalization does seem to facilitate simultaneous motor responses (Tinsley & Waters, 1982), it appears that overt verbalization does not generally facilitate cognitive performance. Some studies have found that overt self-verbalizations can interfere with the performance of 4- and 5-year-old children (Denney, 1975; Meichenbaum & Goodman, 1969) and others have found that overt self-verbalization is no more effective than adults' instructions regarding successful performance strategies (Bronckart, 1973; Denney & Turner, 1979).

Despite the facilitative effects of verbal mediation and verbal mnemonic processes, the view that language and speech inhibit cognition has been widespread.

Cognition Inhibited by Language

It is commonly assumed that language inhibits thought; any given language, in this view, provides, by its vocabulary and grammar, a specific set of cognitive and perceptual distinctions and relationships. Thus, as a child learns a native language, the child's thought is shaped or molded by that language's vocabulary and grammar. As a result, the child's thought comes to be increasingly constrained by these linguistic categories and relations so that the thought of the adult is severely limited. We shall review two consequences of this linguistic inhibition of cognition: childhood amnesia and linguistic determinism.

Childhood Amnesia

Why are adults unable to recall many childhood experiences? Memories of early childhood experiences are generally inaccessible, whereas memories of adolescence and adulthood can be retrieved (Linton, 1975, 1982). Few adults are able to recall events from their early childhood, such as their first birthday party or the birth of a younger sibling (Sheingold & Tenney, 1982; Waldvogel, 1982).

Schachtel (1959) argued that early autobiographical memories are inaccessible because of the later acquisition of language. Thus, language inhibits memory because the acquisition of a first language provides the child with a set of concepts and relations that are alien to those initially used to organize and represent experience. The adult's recall is limited to those experiences that can be verbalized; the events of childhood were not encoded and stored in terms of the linguistic concepts adults use to direct memory search and retrieval.

Several studies have indeed documented the growth with age in the number of memories recalled by adults. For example, Dudycha and Dudycha (1933) found that the earliest documented memory of adolescent males was of events that occurred when they were 3.67 years of age and that of adolescent females was of events that occurred at 3.50 years. Waldvogel (1982) found that his male subjects recalled an average of 0.18 memories of the period from birth to 3 years but recalled 16.17 memories of their seventh year. Waldvogel's female subjects' recall was slightly better; they recalled an average of 0.33 memories from their first 3 years and 16.67 memories from their seventh year. Sheingold and Tenney (1982) interviewed college students about the events surrounding the birth of a younger sibling. Age at the time of the birth, rather the elapsed time, was the better predictor of how well the students could recall, e.g., "Who took care of you while your mother was at the hospital?" or "What presents did the baby get?" Students who were under the age of 3 at the time of the sibling's birth recalled essentially nothing about the birth, although more than half of the 20 questions were answered by students who were 3 to 5 years old at the time of the sibling's birth.

Linguistic Determinism

The assumed inhibitory effects of language extend beyond those of childhood amnesia. In this century, Whorf (1956) is the most widely known proponent of the view that language inhibits adult perception and cognition. (See Schaff, 1973, for a discussion of the history of linguistic determinism.) In 1940 Whorf argued:

> The background linguistic system (in other words, the grammar) of each language . . . is itself the shaper of ideas, the program and guide for the individual's mental activity, for his analysis of impressions, for his synthesis of his mental stock in trade. . . . We cut nature up . . . largely because we are partners in an agreement to organize it in this way . . . [as] codified in the patterns of our language. (1956, pp. 212–213)

Whorf believed that support for his view of linguistic determinism is self-evident in vocabulary and grammatical differences. As examples, Whorf pointed to (1) the "timelessness" of the Hopi verb inflectional system, which does not mark "the present, past, and future of the event itself but . . . what type of validity the speaker intends the statement to have" (p. 217), and (2) the remarkable ability of North American Eskimo to distinguish different types of snow, as indicated by their many different words for snow, in contrast to the presumed inability of Aztecs to distinguish between snow, ice, and slush given their single word for frozen water.

Discussion

Despite the widespread appeal of Whorf's views on the inhibitory effects of language, there is little actual empirical support for linguistic determinism. As reviewed by Foss and Hakes (1978), Slobin (1979), and Steinberg (1982), attempts to demonstrate actual perceptual or cognitive impairments resulting from limitations of vocabulary or grammar have been unsuccessful (but see Bloom, 1981). Nor is Whorf's argument supported by his own examples.

Consider but one counterargument to linguistic determinism. Whorf expressly pointed to the role of language in shaping concepts of time. Whorf believed that English speakers, as well as those who speak other standard, European languages such as French and German, conceive of time as a smoothly flowing continuum of past-present-future. Whorf argued that this conception of time results from the verb inflectional system that distinguishes past, present, and future by forming three tenses. However, as pointed out by Chomsky (1973) and Palmer (1976), English, as well as other standard European languages, does not have a tripartite division of tenses. Rather, we convey a sense of past, present, and future by using verb inflections for tense, aspect, and modality, respectively. The past tense distinguishes temporally remote events from all others, the progressive aspect marks continuous or habitual events, and the future likelihood of an event is not uniquely distinguished from the other modalities of permission, ability, necessity, and obligation. Speakers of English thus have a conception of a past-present-future time continuum superimposed on the English inflectional system for remote-continuous-likely events, so Whorf's hypothesis is not supported by his own example.

In contrast, Schachtel's account of childhood amnesia is widely accepted. Childhood memories are rare and the decline in memories of childhood does seem to be associated with the later stages of language acquisition. Of course, the development of language is confounded with the development of other cognitive skills and abilities and the studies of childhood amnesia make no attempt to separate out linguistic effects from other developmental effects. This research also offers no explanation of why females have better recall of childhood events than males. Furthermore, it leads to the rather odd prediction that those persons who do not acquire language would have total, unhampered recall of childhood experiences. Of course, given the reliance on verbal report as a measure of recall, it would be difficult to determine if that were the case.

Thus, candidates for inhibitory effects of language acquisition on cognitive development lack convincing support based on empirical findings. Childhood amnesia does occur and is linked, although not conclusively, with language acquisition. Linguistic determinism, of the strong form advocated by Whorf, is supported neither by Whorf's own examples or by research on the effects of vocabulary and grammatical differences on perception and cognition.

Conclusions

As children master the grammar and vocabulary of their native language, they acquire a set of verbal labels and category terms for objects and relations. At the same time, children gradually learn to use these vocabulary items to regulate behavior, mediate perceptual responses, and encode, organize, and retrieve information. Language acquisition both facilitates and inhibits cognition as a result of both the acquisition of grammar and vocabulary and the acquisition of regulatory, mediational, and mnemonic processes. Language acquisition can facilitate cognition by equipping children with the semantic knowledge necessary to understand complex instructions, the verbal responses needed to describe perceptual principles, and the verbal mnemonics required to encode, organize, and retrieve information. Language acquisition can inhibit cognition by making children dependent upon these verbal mnemonics and, possibly, thereby impairing the retrieval of nonverbal information such as memories of childhood.

The pervasiveness of linguistic influences on cognition is limited by two factors: First, in order to influence cognition, linguistic labels and categories must be used to mediate perception and to facilitate memory. Second, not all thought is verbal or propositional; nonverbal, analogue processes have been proposed as alternatives and supplements to verbal ones.

The use of available verbal mediators and verbal mnemonics is not inevitable. Children and adults in nontechnological societies are less reliant on verbal encoding and categorization than their counterarts in urbanized and technological societies (Cole, Gay, Glick, & Sharp, 1971; Cole & Scribner, 1981; Luria, 1976; Scribner & Cole, 1972). Luria observed that nonliterate adults may not use available verbal mediators to describe, categorize, and organize perceptual arrays. Cole and his colleagues have observed that adults in nonliterate and nonurbanized societies, like young children in the United States, may have production deficits that limit how they use linguistic information to aid memory. Despite the availability of terms for objects, relations, and categories, adults in nontechnological societies may not label objects or arrays, rehearse the labels, categorize the labels, and use categorical retrieval strategies. Hence, facilitative effects of language and cognition will not be observed because verbal mediators and verbal mnemonics, although available, are not actually used to learn and remember information.

Verbal mediators and verbal mnemonics are not the only means to encode and organize information. Nonverbal, analogue processes can be used to compare objects, encode relations, and remember facts (Cooper & Shepard, 1973; Kosslyn, 1980; Paivio & Begg, 1981). Analogue perceptual and mnemonic processes may be used in lieu of verbal processes or may be used to supplement verbal ones. Consequently, inhibitory effects of language on cognition may be offset by the effects of analogue perceptual and mnemonic processes. Analogue processes may compensate for the limitations of grammar and vocabulary and, thus, prevent inhibitory effects such as those proposed by Whorf and other advocates of linguistic determinism. In a similar fashion, analogue processes may be called upon by persons who do not have grammar or vocabulary available for use.

To the extent that language facilitates cognitive functioning, children who are unable to master language, or who do so in an irregular manner, are doubly handicapped: they have a limited means of communicating their thoughts to others, and they have limited access to potentially powerful mental tools. The facilitative effects of language discussed above depend upon the child's ability to use appropriate words to regulate behavior, to label perceptual distinctions, or to encode and retrieve information. Yet many children with language-learning problems have word-finding difficulties (Wiig, Semel, & Nystrom, 1982). Unless these children are able to improvise analogue or nonlinguistic codes to serve as mediators or mnemonic devices, they will be at a disadvantage compared to peers who have words to serve in those capacities. Highly verbal activities, such as reading, are obviously ones that involve double jeopardy. However, the secondary limitation of a language disability may influence children's performance on nonlinguistic tasks as well (Siegel et al., 1981). As we noted earlier, when discussing the interaction hypothesis, there is a possibility of secondary effects. Some have argued that language-disordered children have more pervasive problems of mental representation that account for their language acquisition difficulties. However, their limited performance on some nonlinguistic tests may be a function of reduced access to verbal cognitive tools helpful in solving the nonlinguistic tasks.

Chapter 7

Overview,
Conclusions,
Projections, and
Synthesis

Overview

We have reviewed, summarized, criticized, and extended the contemporary literature regarding the relationship between children's language acquisition and their cognitive development. We started with some fundamental distinctions; chief among them is the assertion that language and cognition are not isomorphic. Given this assertion, it follows that the child's task in learning language is establishing linkages between language and cognition: a mapping problem confronts children, who must master the meanings of words and the use of morphological and syntactic devices. A second corollary of the nonisomorphism of cognition and language is that not all aspects of language need have cognitive correlates. Therefore, children must master some linguistic conventions that are autonomous, arbitrary, and unique to language.

We discussed various solutions and revisions of the mapping problem across the span of language acquisition, from the emergence of words in infancy to the mastery of complex syntactic constructions and metalinguistic judgments in late childhood. In Chapters 2 and 3 we described the rich contemporary debates focusing on the earliest beginnings of language. Six accounts of the relationship between language and cognition were described: the strong and weak cognition hypotheses, the local homologies hypothesis, the interaction account, the cognition-anchored-in-language hypothesis, and the language-specific/perceptual processes hypothesis. These accounts differ in the cognitive and linguistic skills examined, and in the level of development studied.

We argued that existing models must be extended to include additional kinds of linguistic and cognitive development, and cognition-language relationships evident beyond the early stages of development. In Chapter 4, we proposed three additional components of cognition relevant to language acquisition: person knowledge, social categories, and event knowledge. In Chapter 5 we argued that, with advanced linguistic knowledge, additional cognitive abilities come into play: mature cognitive operations, such as reversibility and conservation, cognitive strategies, including probablistic and perceptual strategies and inductive heuristics, and metalinguistic judgments. Another consequence of advanced language acquisition is the use of language to regulate behavior, mediate perceptual processes, and encode, organize, and retrieve information. In Chapter 6 we concluded that language can both facilitate and inhibit mental functioning.

A final retrospective observation is that the empirical base for the literature consists of diverse kinds of evidence, collected with a variety of methods. Data may be collected from in-depth case studies, longitudinal studies of small numbers of children, cross-sectional studies of children from different ages, or comparative studies of normal and language-impaired or cognitively impaired children. Also the data may be based on samples of spontaneous or elicited speech production, experimental tests of comprehension, or metalinguistic judgments of acceptability, synonymity, and so forth.

Conclusions

Our major conclusion is that there is no one, general, pervasive relationship between children's nonlinguistic and linguistic knowledge. Instead, there is a network of tenuous linkages between localized areas of cognitive and linguistic knowledge. Furthermore, the direction of influence varies from one linkage to another; cognitive development can influence language acquisition, yet language may affect cognition. The types of linkages shift with the child's ontogenetic development. In effect, the structure of linkages is four-dimensional. It depends on:

1. The nature of the cognitive competencies involved
2. The nature of the linguistic competencies involved
3. The level of mental development involved
4. The nature of the tasks and evidence

Conclusions about the relationship of language and cognition are, consequently, tentative and depend on the particular combinations of linguistic and cognitive competencies, developmental levels, and tasks of interest.

As we examine these conclusions, we can project some expansions or adjustments of present models. We begin with a discussion of the dependence of the first two dimensions, the nature of cognitive and linguistic competencies, on available theoretical models. Next we discuss the third dimension, developmental level, and offer some projections. Finally, we address the matter of task variables, suggesting that they reflect differences in linkage of cognition and language.

Projections

New Models of Cognition and Language

Theories of linguistic and cognitive competence impose limitations on the study of language acquisition and cognitive development, insofar as they determine where investigators will search for information. The contemporary literature includes a number of challenges to established models of cognition and language. New models promise new perspectives regarding the relationship of language and cognition.

Alternatives to Piaget The dominance of Piaget's model of cognitive development has been evident throughout this volume. We pointed out some of the limitations of this perspective in Chapter 3, in our discussion of concepts beyond the purview of Piaget's theory. As discussed earlier, Piaget's neglect of the social dimensions of development is a major deficiency in accounting for the cognitive underpinnings of language development. Another obvious shortcoming, which we mentioned in Chapter 2, is the Piagetian emphasis on the cognitive deficiencies of children 2 through 7 years of age—the preoperational period. Piaget defines this stage by what children cannot do, their failure on tasks of operational intelligence. In contrast to the rich set of skills he formulated for infants in the sensorimotor stage, there are few cognitive constructs proposed for the preoperational period. An investigator planning to tie cognitive achievements with linguistic milestones during this time of rapid and rich language acquisition is hard pressed to find particular tasks in the Piagetian literature. The constructs of seriation, reversibility, and class inclusion account for almost all the investigations with children of this age.

In addition to criticisms based on Piaget's omissions, a growing group of developmental psychologists argue that Piaget was incorrect in some of his fundamental assumptions. Two of these assumptions have particular relevance for the cognition/language debate. One assumption is that the child's mind is structurally different from that of the adult; another is that ontogenetic cognitive development proceeds in stages, characterized by pervasive patterns of linkage across cognitive domains.

Do children start with a structured intellect with which they come to know the world, or do they build a mind as they acquire knowledge? Piaget asserted that the child's mind is structurally different from that of the adult. Fodor (1979) countered this view by arguing that the child is in the paradoxical position of acquiring more powerful cognitive structures from weaker ones. Fodor claims that this is a logically implausible accomplishment. Furthermore, such a position presumes given mental abilities powerful enough to construct a mind as a function of experience. Thus, the child's mind must initially include cognitive structure.

Scholars such as Fodor, Donaldson (1977), and Macnamara (1982) believe that it is more parsimonious to assume that children's minds come with ready-made cognitive structures. They call upon evidence documenting infants' perceptual and conceptual abilities, and heretofore unrecognized adult-like cognitive abilities of young children, such as early logical abilities (e.g., Macnamara, 1977; Macnamara, Baker, & Olson, 1976; Pea, 1982). These abilities appear to be independent of experience and so demonstrate that children's minds are cognitively structured like those of adults.

A model of cognition that grants adult intellectual structures to children's minds is clearly compatible with the idea of innate, language-specific intellectual mechanisms. Within this account, children do not "learn" language in the traditional sense. Instead, language acquisition is a matter of the unfolding of predetermined levels. The unfolding of language may be principled and orderly with respect to specialization and restriction of maturing competencies. Children call upon innate categories and linguistic processing principles powerful enough to construct language and constrained enough not to construct idiosyncratic linguistic structures. Such a view of intellectual development diminishes the role of general cognitive heuristics in the acquisition of language. The extent to which this model of mental structure is accepted will influence the amount of future support for the language-specific processes hypothesis.

A second kind of alternative to Piaget dispenses with the idea of stage development and its corollary, pervasive linkages across cognitive domains. A fully formulated statement of this position is presented by Fischer (1980), who assumes that in all domains children acquire situation-specific skills. Their mastery of skills is uneven across domains. Instead of a general stage unity across tasks, unevenness in acquisition is the rule. Skill theory has specific implications for accounts of language acquisition (Fischer & Corrigan, 1981). Language and cognition comprise sets of specific skills that are interrelated in localized linkages. Cognition is not separate from language. Therefore, one cannot be a prerequisite for the other, in any general sense. Within this view of children's development, a general characterization of the relationship between cognition and language is impossible, as is a statement about general cognitive or linguistic knowledge. Instead, knowledge, whether linguistic or cognitive, is task dependent.

One advantage of the skill theory is that it addresses the intellectual growth between 10 months and 5 years of age, a time of rapid language growth. Fischer (1980) proposed a sequence of 10 successive optimal levels of skill mastery from infancy to adulthood. The skill levels are organized into three tiers: sensorimotor, representational, and abstract. The span for 10 months to 5 years encompasses skill levels 3 to 5, and the shift from the sensorimotor to the representational tier. Fischer and Corrigan (1981) described the course of language acquisition through the associated skill levels.

A disadvantage of skill theory is that description of a complex, multifaceted ability such as language entails analysis of many different levels of skills. Fischer and Corrigan provide a general sketch of the language skills associated with the cognitive levels of the preschool years, along with a detailed skill analysis of a few particular linguistic accomplishments. The analyses that they provide raise a number of questions and are certain to provoke counterarguments. It is not clear how the particulars of local skills are to be characterized, or how the skills interrelate with each other. Nevertheless, skill theory provides an interesting alternative to Piaget's model.

New Linguistic Perspectives   Just as the contemporary debate about cognition and language draws on Piagetian theory for characterizations of children's cognitive development, Chomsky has provided the dominant model of language. A central notion is that of linguistic transformations, which have been linked with Piaget's cognitive operations. Linguistic transformations were proposed by Chomsky as a formal means of mapping deep linguistic structures onto alternative surface forms. Transformations, such as passivization or wh-fronting, typically move, delete, or add linguistic elements. They are governed by formally specified constraints that are considered to be universal in their application. Piagetian operations also serve a transforming function, relating one arrangement of objects to another. These operations, such as reversibility or conservation, are governed by formal principles, e.g., identity or negation, that ensure their correct application. Given these obvious parallels between Chomskian transformations and Piagetian operations, it is not surprising that students of child language acquisition attempted to link the acquisition of one to the development of the other. As discussed in Chapter 5, Cromer, Beilin, Tremaine, and others have suggested that the acquisition of verb tense, mood, aspect, and voice as well as the acquisition of particular syntactic forms is contingent on the prior mastery of cognitive operations, including reversibility and conservation.

Yet such a theory linking the acquisition of transformationally derived structures to cognitive development is necessarily constrained by the assumption of the psychological reality of linguistic transformations. Recently, the notion of linguistic transformation has been questioned by proponents of lexical-functional grammars. Bresnan and her colleagues (Bresnan, 1982a, 1982b; Kaplan & Bresnan, 1982) have radically reformulated generative grammars so as to weaken the notion of transformations. No longer are alternative surface forms such as active and passive sentences generated from a common deep structure by different transformations. Rather, different lexical entries for active and passive verbs are assumed. The entries specify both the syntactic structures into which the verbs can be inserted and the functional roles of noun phrases in those structures. The active form specifies a noun phrase as the subject of the verb that is also the agent of the action. The passive form specifies a noun phrase as the subject of the verb that is also the object of the action. Lexical redundancy rules capture similarities across different lexical entries.

Lexical-functional grammars have been espoused as models of language acquisition by Pinker (1982) and Maratsos (1978). With their emphasis on lexical rules and "close to the surface" syntactic structures, lexical-functional grammars are compatible with the work on the acquisition of syntactic form classes via distributional and semantic analysis. Given the assumptions of lexical-functional grammars, parallels between Piagetian cognitive operations and syntactic transformations cannot be maintained and, hence, attempts to link the acquisition of particular transformational forms to the development of particular cognitive operations are no longer viable.

Developmental Level

There are two major ontogenetic changes in the relationship between cognition and language: one is a shift in the relative amounts of linguistic and cognitive knowledge and the other is an alternation in the nature of the available knowledge. In regard to the first, it is self-evident that babies first acquire knowledge about their world, and only somewhat farther along in their development do they begin to master language. Ontogenetically, cognition precedes language. If we restrict our perspective to the individual child, it is reasonable to conclude that the direction of influence must be from cognition to language. Knowledge worked out on a nonlinguistic level precedes acquisition of the linguistic means of communicating it. Indeed, much of the evidence in support of the strong cognition and local homologies accounts is from the earliest stages of acquisition (see Table 1). However, if we broaden our perspective to include the language and behaviors of the child's interlocutors, we see bidirectional influences. The child draws upon inductive heuristics and cognitive strategies to infer the symbolic value of his own utterances and the comments of others. Toddlers formulate some tentative hypotheses about cognition that are in turn altered (interaction hypothesis) or stabilized (cognition-anchored-in-language hypothesis) by the inferences they draw from the verbal and social responses of other speakers. The child's initial cognitive knowledge is a bootstrap for subsequently acquired word meanings and rudimentary linguistic rules; language expands and enriches this initial knowledge.

Further along in development, a child masters the basics of vocabulary, syntax, contextual adjustments, discourse, and metalinguisitic judgment. Here again, the relationship between language and cognition shifts. Now, linguistic knowledge has become a powerful intellectual tool. Children can continue to generate nonlinguistic hypotheses to be tested against linguistic regularities. They now, however, have other options. They can use linguistic knowledge as a tool for the acquisition of new nonlinguistic concepts or structures, yet they must overcome inhibiting effects of existing linguistic knowledge to master new cognitive skills. Language now exerts powerful influences on cognition.

Along with the ontogenetic shift in the direction of influence are ontogenetic changes in linguistic and cognitive knowledge. Initially, the child's problem is to discover the links between communicative intentions and words. Children call upon psychological primitives in order to accomplish this match. In addition to sensorimotor knowledge, they may have available a set of inherent psychological predispositions, such as perceptual mechanisms especially tuned to speech regularities, an inherent organization of the world that corresponds to the basic lexical categories, a fundamental sense of reference for word-object relationships, and social and emotional distinctions and groupings. Later on, children must learn rules for the use of word order and word endings; at that time they call upon other cognitive and linguistic competencies. Among the candidates are probablistic strategies, inductive heuristics, and language-specific operating principles. Still later, their emerging logical capacities allow for the full formulation of logical operations and associated mastery of linguistic terms and formal syntactic conventions. The cognitive ability to consider several dimensions of a problem simultaneously and to separate one's personal perspective from the problem is associated with the development of metalinguistic judgments of linguistic forms and meanings.

We conclude that there is a reduction in the relative contribution of cognition to language with ontogenetic development, an increase in the relative role of language in cognitive development and concomitantly, an increase in the sophistication of the two domains. Along with these two ontogenetic shifts is a broadening and complication of the nature of linkages between language and cognition. Indeed, as children develop they seem to search for such linkages, as is evident in the preschooler's use of *Why?* as a means of expanding sensorimotor understandings (Blank, 1974) and the elementary-age child's search for the formal scientific name for a new butterfly, or the proper word for discussing private bodily functions in public.

Conclusions about the relationship between cognition and language depend upon the ontogenetic level studied. At early levels, cognition dominates language; at later levels language and cognition are balanced. At early levels, few linkages between cognition and language are apparent; at later levels multiple, bidirectional, and branching linkages between language and cognitive have developed.

Task Variables

There are inherent psychological differences across various linguistic and cognitive tasks. Some of the apparent discrepancies in the cognition and language relationship across tasks may be actual rather than artifactual. A case in point is the difference between tasks involving the production and those involving the comprehension of language. Studies in which cognitive measures are correlated separately with production and comprehension measures report patterns of correlation between cognitive measures and language comprehension that are different from those between cognitive measures and production (Bates, 1979; Smolak, 1982).

Evidence from a study of children's color term acquisition (Rice, 1980) suggested that such apparent discrepancies reflect differences in the retrieval of cognitive information in the two modalities. Preschool children were trained to label the colors of objects. At the completion of production training, some children performed correctly on comprehension tasks whereas others did not. The difference between groups was associated with what they knew about color on a nonlinguistic level prior to training. Children who spontaneously mastered comprehension were those who sorted objects according to color prior to training, that is, those having a nonlinguistic category that corresponded to the color terms to be taught. Those children who could correctly label the colors of objects but not select the appropriate color when asked to do so were children who did not sort by color prior to training. Rice (1980, 1984a) argued that the memory demands for production and comprehension tasks are such that a child can produce words with less complete cognitive knowledge than that required for a comprehension task. Evidently production tasks tap into underlying cognitive knowledge at a level different from that tapped by comprehension tasks.

The extent to which the cognition and language relationship may be task dependent warrants further investigation. The possibility of such task dependence is consistent with Fischer and Corrigan's emphasis on task-dependent skill structures. If this is the case, it will require substantive revision of existing models and axioms of language acquisition. Some familiar assumptions will have to be scrapped. One is the supposition that comprehension always precedes production. Another is the presumption that conclusions based on children's linguistic productions will generalize to their comprehension competencies.

Synthesis: A Model of Language Growth

Language is a network of interrelated skills that is multiply determined. At least three separate sources are involved in language acquisition: innate cognitive and linguistic competencies, general cognitive strategies and heuristics, and conceptual knowledge.

A child's mastery of language may be likened to the growth of a plant (Figure 6). In the original seed are the innate cognitive and linguistic propensities; these are the infant's sprouting perceptions of the verbal behavior of others and the sprout's early nourishment. The first growth is the establishment of a root system, the conceptual knowledge that supports language and grows as the child develops. The child draws upon the conceptual roots and the innate kernel to establish the first green shoots of language. As the shoots develop, they provide further nourishment to strengthen the delicate young conceptual roots. In turn, as the roots firm and expand, they provide support and nourishment for the developing plant. The initial kernel continues to contribute to growth, perhaps through the timed release of growth hormones that stimulate root and leaf development. The stem, branches, and leaves of a plant are shaped by the plant's ecology and evolution. So, too, the syntactic structures, semantic content, and pragmatics of language are responsive both to the child's environment and heredity.

As the human language plant grows, it manifests some unusual properties. It anticipates the probability of events and other regularities of the world. It is aware of its own growth and structure. As a consequence its growth can appear to be out of phase, with premature growth of some branches and relative stunting of other branches. Plant growth is governed by geotropic and heliotropic responses to gravity and light. In the same way, the growth of language is shaped by general cognitive strategies and heuristics. These strategies interrelate previous experiences and knowledge with present and future situations.

In normally developing children, language matures in a balanced manner. There is a symmetry of shape and structural composition; the system is flexible and responsive to its environment. Healthy language reflects an equilibrium among the three sources

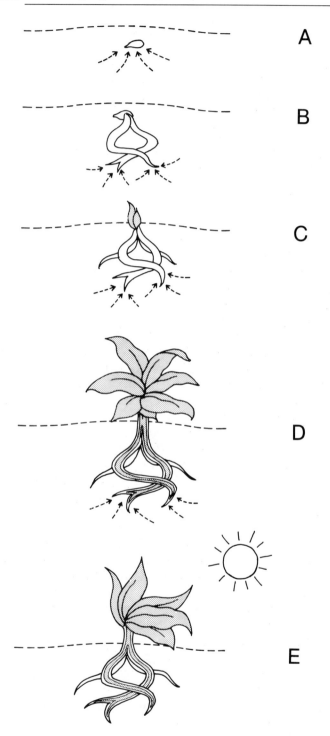

A

B

C

D

E

of growth, the kernel of innate propensities, the roots of cognition, and the stem, branches, and leaves of syntax, semantics, and pragmatics.

For some children, the language plant does not thrive. Normal growth is prevented by deficits in one or more contributing sources. The meagre language skills of mentally retarded children are evidence of a limited root structure and perhaps limited nutrients in the initial kernel. A stunted language plant is the result.

This metaphor can be applied also to language-disordered and autistic children. Such children appear to lack cognitive strategies and heuristics for inducing grammatical rules, yet they seem to possess intact cognitive and linguistic predispositions and adequate conceptual knowledge. Under such circumstances, these children must rely more heavily on the intact sources of linguistic information than might normal children. Such an imbalance would lead to an uneven pattern of linguistic skills and abilities. A heavy reliance on cognitive knowledge may contribute to learning those aspects of language directly mapped onto underlying meanings, but may interfere with mastery of arbitrary linguistic rules. Furthermore, the imbalance will have ontogenetic consequences. The plant may have disproportionate growth in one area, such as the stem, with little growth in other areas, such as few leaves, or the overall growth may be stunted. To the extent that language skills are restricted, they are unavailable as cognitive tools. Children who are linguistically impaired are likely to be unable to formulate and use verbal strategies in order to regulate their own behavior, or to use verbal mnemonic processes to encode, organize, and retrieve new conceptual information.

There are many other ways in which the language acquisition process may be imbalanced. Each of the three sources is a candidate for deficiencies. The ultimate consequence of a particular deficiency depends upon its contribution to language relative to the

---

Figure 6 A model of a child's language growth. (*A*): Original seed—innate cognitive and linguistic propensities, nourished by environmental nutrients, serve as the basis for language. (*B*): First growth—linguistic knowledge is preceded by the establishment of a root system of conceptual knowledge. (*C*): First language—beginnings of the language "plant" emerge from innate and cognitive underpinnings. (*D*): Functional language—emergent language skills provide nourishment to innate and conceptual roots, which in turn continue to contribute to linguistic growth. (*E*): Language strategies—language growth is shaped by cognitive strategies and heuristics that interact with the probability of events and regularities of the world.

other sources and the ontogenetic level of concern. Some deficiencies, such as limited cognitive strategies and heuristics, may have pervasive consequences, whereas other deficiencies, such as lack of particular conceptual knowledge, may be more restricted in influence.

Language acquisition is an organic process like the growth of a plant. Language is acquired, stored, and used by a living person. Mastery of language is dynamic and variable. The rate of acquisition is most rapid during early childhood, slows during late childhood and early adolescence, and then continues at a steady pace throughout the remaining lifetime. Language is an intimate part of the more general mental, emotional, and physical growth of an individual.

The demands of contemporary empirical behavior science lead to the compartmentalization of aspects of children's development. The study of child language has emerged as a special area of scholarship, beside areas such as cognitive development and social development. Once these divisions are made, they acquire a reality of their own. As a consequence, scholars study either children's language or cognition or social development.

The recent effort to interrelate cognition and language is an attempt to understand the organic interaction inherent in children's development. The connections between cognition and language are strong and rich. The plant metaphor captures the systemic, dynamic, and interactive character of the interrelationship. The metaphor is limited, however, insofar as it represents only a few aspects of language and general development, albeit the centrally important ones.

The immediate challenge is to build metaphors and models that are comprehensive in scope and yet capture the elegant internal cohesion of the human language acquisition system. Such attempts further our understanding of the ordinary miracle of language. Furthermore, representative metaphors and models add to our ability to identify the factors that contribute to the disruption of normal language skills and the procedures with which a basic communicative competence can be built.

References

Abelson, R. P. Psychological status of the script concept. *American Psychologist,* 1981, *36(7),* 715–729.

Altshuler, K. The social and psychological development of the deaf child: Problems, their treatment and prevention. *American Annals of the Deaf,* 1974, *117,* 365–376.

Anderson, D. R., Alwitt, L. F., Lorch, E. P., & Levin, S. R. Watching children watch television. In G. Hall & M. Lewis (Eds.), *Attention and the development of cognitive skills.* New York: Plenum, 1979.

Anderson, E. *Learning to speak with style: A study of the sociolinguistic skills of children.* Unpublished doctoral dissertation, 1977, Stanford University.

Anglin, J. *Word, object and conceptual development.* New York: Norton, 1977.

Atkinson, R. C., Hansen, D. N., & Bernbach, H. Short-term memory with young children. *Psychonomic Science,* 1964, *1,* 255–256.

Atkinson, R. C., & Shiffrin, R. M. Human memory: A proposed system and its control processes. In K. W. Spence & J. T. Spence (Eds.), *The psychology of learning* (Vol. 2). New York: Academic Press, 1968.

Bartlett, E. J. The acquisition of the meaning of color terms: A study of lexical development. In R. N. Campbell & P. T. Smith (Eds.), *Proceedings of the NATO Conference on the psychology of language.* New York: Plenum, 1978.

Bates, E. *Language and context: The acquisition or pragmatics.* New York: Academic Press, 1976.

Bates, E. *The emergence of symbols: Cognition and communication in infancy.* New York: Academic Press, 1979.

125

Bates, E., Benigni, L., Bretherton, I., Camaioni, L., & Volterra, V. From gesture to the first word: On cognitive and social prerequisites. In M. Lewis & L. Rosenblum (Eds.), *Interaction, conversation, and the development of language.* New York: John Wiley and Sons, 1977, 247–307.

Bates, E., Bretherton, I., Beeghly-Smith, M., & McNew, J. Social bases of language development: A reassessment. In H. W. Reese & L. P. Lipsitt (Eds.), *Advances in child development and behavior,* (Vol. 16). New York: Academic Press, 1982.

Bates, E., Camaioni, L., & Volterra, V. The acquisition of performatives prior to speech. *Merrill-Palmer Quarterly,* 1975, *21*(3), 205–226.

Bates, E., & Snyder, L. The cognitive hypothesis in language development. In I. Uzgiris & J. McV. Hunt (Eds.), *Research with scales of psychological development in infancy.* Champaign-Urbana, Ill.: University of Illinois Press, 1982.

Beilin, H. *Studies in the cognitive basis of language development.* New York: Academic Press, 1975.

Belmont, J. M., & Butterfield, E. C. The relation of short-term memory to development and intelligence. In L. C. Lipsitt & H. W. Reese (Ed.), *Advances in child development and behavior* (Vol. 4). New York: Academic Press, 1969.

Bever, T. G. The cognitive basis of linguistic structures. In J. B. Hayes (Ed.), *Cognition and the development of language.* New York: Wiley, 1970.

Bever, T. G., Fodor, J. A., & Weskel, W. Is linguistics empirical? *Psychological Review,* 1965, *72,* 493–500. (a)

Bever, T. G., Fodor, J. A., & Weskel, W. On the acquisition of syntax. *Psychological Review,* 1965, *72,* 467–482. (b)

Bickerton, D. *Roots of language.* Ann Arbor, Mich.: Karoma, 1981.

Bickerton, D. Learning without experience the Creole way. In L. Obler & L. Menn (Eds.), *Exceptional language and linguistics.* New York: Academic Press, 1982.

Bickerton, D. Creole languages. *Scientific American,* 1983, *249,* 116–122.

Billow, R. A cognitive development study of metaphor comprehension. *Developmental Psychology,* 1975, *11,* 415–423.

Blank, M. Cognitive functions of language in the preschool years. *Developmental Psychology,* 1974, *10,* 229–245.

Bloom, A. *The linguistic shaping of thought: Study of the impact of language on thinking in China and the West.* Hillsdale, N.J.: Erlbaum Associates, 1981.

Bloom, L. *Language development: Form and function in emerging grammars.* Cambridge, Mass.: MIT Press, 1970.

Bloom, L. *One word at a time: The use of single-word utterances before syntax.* The Hague: Mouton, 1973.

Bloom, L., Lahey, M., Hood, L., Lifter, K., & Fiess, K. Complex sentences: Acquisition of syntactic connectives and the semantic relations they encode. *Journal of Child Language,* 1980, *7,* 235–261.

Bloom, L., Lightbown, R., & Hood, L. Structure and variation in child language. *Monographs of the Society for Research in Child Development,* 1975, *40*(2, Serial No. 160).

Bohannon, J. N. The relationship between syntax discrimination, imitation, and comprehension. *Child Development,* 1975, *46,* 444–451.

Bohannon, J. N. Normal and scrambled grammar in discrimination, imitation, and comprehension. *Child Development,* 1976, *47,* 669–681.

Bornstein, M. H. Color vision and color naming: A psychophysiological hypothesis of cultural difference. *Psychological Bulletin,* 1973, *80,* 257–285.

Botvin, G. J., & Sutton-Smith, B. The development of structural complexity in children's fantasy narratives. *Developmental Psychology,* 1977, *13,* 377–388.

Bowerman, M. *Early syntactic development: A cross-lingusitic study with special reference to Finnish.* London: Cambridge University Press, 1973.

Bowerman, M. Learning the structure of causative verbs: A study in the relationship of cognitive, semantic, and syntactic development. *Papers and Reports on Child Language* (Stanford University), 1974, *8,* 142–178.

Bowerman, M. Semantic factors in the acquisition of rules for word use and sentence construction. In D. Morehead & A. Morehead (Eds.), *Directions in normal and deficient child language.* Baltimore: University Park Press, 1976.

Bowerman, M. The acquisition of word meaning: An investigation into some current conflicts. In N. Waterson & C. Snow (Eds.), *The development of communication.* Chichester, England: John Wiley, 1978. (a)

Bowerman, M. Semantic and syntactic development: A review of what, when, and how in language acquisition. In R. L. Schiefelbusch (Ed.), *Bases of language intervention.* Baltimore: University Park Press, 1978. (b)

Bowerman, M. Cross-cultural perspectives on language development. In H. C. Triandis & A. Heron (Eds.), *Handbook of cross-cultural psychology* (Vol. 4). Boston: Allyn & Bacon, 1981.

Bowerman, M. The child's expression of meaning: Expanding relationships among lexicon, syntax, and morphology. In H. Winitz (Ed.), *Native language and foreign language acquisition.* New York: New York Academy of Sciences, 1982. (a)

Bowerman, M. Reorganizational processes in language development. In L. R. Gleitman & E. Wanner (Eds.), *Language acquisition: The state of the art.* London: Cambridge University Press, 1982. (b)

Braine, M. D. S. On learning the grammatical order of words. *Psychological Review,* 1963, *79,* 323–348.

Braine, M. D. S. Children's first word combinations. *Monographs of the Society for Research in Child Development,* 1976, *41* (1, Serial No. 164).

Brainerd, C. J. *Piaget's theory of intelligence.* Englewood Cliffs, N.J.: Prentice-Hall, 1978.

Braunwald, S. R. Context, word and meaning: Toward a communicational analysis of lexical acquisition. In A. Lock (Ed.), *Action, gesture, and symbol: The emergence of language.* New York: Academic Press, 1978.

Bresnan, J. Control and complementation. In J. Bresnan (Ed.), *The mental representation of grammatical relations.* Cambridge, Mass.: MIT Press, 1982. (a)

Bresnan, J. The passive in lexical theory. In J. Bresnan (Ed.), *The mental representation of grammatical relations.* Cambridge, Mass.: MIT Press, 1982. (b)

Bretherton, I., McNew, S., & Beeghly-Smith, M. Early person knowledge as expressed in gestural and verbal communication: When do infants acquire a "theory of mind?" In M. E. Lamb & L. R. Sherrod (Eds.), *Infant social cognition.* Hillsdale, N.J.: Erlbaum Associates, 1981.

Bricker, W., & Bricker, D. An early language training strategy. In R. Schiefelbusch & L. Lloyd (Eds.), *Language perspectives: Acquisition, retardation, and intervention.* Baltimore: University Park Press, 1974.

Bronckart, J. P. The regulating role of speech. *Human Development,* 1973, *16,* 417–439.

Brown, A. L., Campione, J. C., Bray, N. W., & Wilcox, B. L. Keeping track of changing variables: Effects of rehearsal training and rehearsal prevention in normal and retarded adolescents. *Journal of Experimental Psychology,* 1973, *101,* 123–131.

Brown, R. *A first language: The early stages.* Cambridge, Mass.: Harvard University Press, 1973.

Brown, R. A new paradigm of reference. In G. A. Miller & E. Lenneberg (Eds.), *Psychology and biology of language and thought:*

Essays in honor of Eric Lenneberg. New York: Academic Press, 1978.

Bruner, J. S., Goodnow, J., & Austin, G. *A study of thinking.* New York: Wiley, 1956.

Butterfield, E. C., & Schiefelbusch, R. L. Some theoretical considerations in the design of language intervention programs. In R. L. Schiefelbusch & D. D. Bricker (Eds.), *Early language: Acquisition and intervention.* Baltimore: University Park Press, 1981, 169–178.

Camarata, S. M., Newhoff, M., & Rugg, B. Perspective taking in normal and language disordered children. In *Proceedings of the symposium on research in children language disorders.* Madison, Wisc.: University of Wisconsin, 1981, 81–88.

Campbell, R. N. Cognitive development and child language. In P. Fletcher & M. Garman (Eds.), *Language acquisition.* Cambridge, England: Cambridge University Press, 1979.

Cantor, N. *Prototypicality and personality judgments.* Unpublished doctoral dissertation, Stanford University, 1978.

Cantor, N., & Mischel, W. Prototypes in person perception. In L. Berkowitz (Ed.), *Advances in experimental social psychology,* (Vol. 12). New York: Academic Press, 1979.

Carey, S. "Less" may never mean more. In R. Campbell & P. T. Smith (Eds.), *Recent advances in the psychology of language: Language development and mother-child interactions.* New York: Plenum, 1978.

Carr, D. B. The development of young children's capacity to judge anomalous sentences. *Journal of Child Language,* 1979, *6,* 227–242.

Cazden, C. *Child language and education.* New York: Holt, Rinehart, & Winston, 1972.

Cazden, C. Play with language and metalinguistic awareness. In C. B. Winsor (Ed.), *Dimensions of language experience.* New York: Agathon Press, 1975.

Chomsky, C. *The acquisition of syntax in children from 5 to 10.* Cambridge, Mass.: MIT Press, 1970.

Chomsky, N. *Syntactic structures.* The Hague: Mouton Publishers, 1957.

Chomsky, N. *Aspects of the theory of syntax.* Cambridge, Mass.: MIT Press, 1965.

Chomsky, N. Introduction. In R. S. Cohen (Ed.), *A. Schaff, Language and cognition.* New York: McGraw-Hill, 1973.

Chomsky, N. *Rules and representations.* New York: Columbia University Press, 1980.

Clark, E. V. Nonlinguistic strategies and the acquisition of word meanings. *Cognition*, 1973, *2*, 161–182. (a)

Clark, E. V. What's in a word? On the child's acquisition of semantics in his first language. In T. E. Moore (Ed.), *Cognitive development and the acquisition of language*. New York: Academic Press, 1973. (b)

Clark, E. V. Knowledge, context, and strategy in the acquisition of meaning. In D. Dato (Ed.), *Developmental psycholinguistics: Theory and applications*. Washington, D. C.: Georgetown University Press, 1975.

Clark, E. V. Strategies and the mapping problem in first language acquisition. In J. Macnamara (Ed.), *Language learning and thought*. New York: Academic Press, 1977, 147–168.

Clark E. V. Here's the top: Nonlinguistic strategies in the acquisition of orientational terms. *Child Development*, 1980, *51*, 329–338.

Clark, H., & Clark, E. *Psychology and language*. New York: Harcourt Brace Jovanovich, 1977.

Cohen, G. *The psychology of cognition*. London: Academic Press, 1977.

Cole, M., Gay, J., Glick, J. A., & Sharp, D. W. *The cultural context of learning and thinking*. New York: Basic Books, 1971.

Cole, M., & Scribner, S. *The psychology of literacy*. Cambridge, Mass.: Harvard University Press, 1981.

Cometa, M. S., & Eson, M. E. Logical operations and metaphor interpretations: A Piagetian model. *Child Development*, 1978, *49*, 649–659.

Cooper, L. A., & Shepard, R. S. Chronometric studies of the rotation of mental images. In W. G. Chase (Ed.), *Visual information processing*. New York: Academic Press, 1973.

Corrigan, R. Language development as related to stage 6 object permanence development. *Journal of Child Language*, 1978, *5*, 173–189.

Corrigan, R. Cognitive correlates of language: Differential criteria yield differential results. *Child Development*, 1979, *50*(3), 617–631.

Corrigan, R. The control of animate and inanimate components in pretend play and language. *Journal of Child Development*, 1982, *53*, 1343–1353.

Cromer, R. F. *The development of temporal reference during the acquisition of language*. Unpublished doctoral dissertation, Harvard University, 1968.

Cromer, R. F. The development of the ability to decenter in time. *British Journal of Psychology*, 1971, *62*, 353–365.

Cromer, R. F. The development of language and cognition: The cognition hypothesis. In B. M. Foss (Ed.), *New perspectives in child development*. Baltimore: Penguin Books, 1974.

Cromer, R. F. The cognitive hypothesis of language acquisition and its implications for child language deficiency. In D. Morehead & A. Morehead (Eds.), *Normal and deficient child language*. Baltimore: University Park Press, 1976.

Cromer, R. F. Reconceptualizing language acquisition and cognitive development. In R. L. Schiefelbusch & D. Bricker (Eds.), *Early language: Acquisition and intervention*. Baltimore: University Park Press, 1981.

Curtiss, S. Developmental dissociation of language and cognition. In L. K. Obler & L. Menn (Eds.), *Exceptional language and linguistics*. New York: Academic Press, 1982, 285–312.

de Ajuriaguerra, J. Speech disorders in childhood. In E. C. Carterette (Ed.), *Brain function: Speech, language, and communication*. Berkeley, Calif.: University of California, 1966.

de Villiers, P. A., & de Villiers, J. G. Early judgments of semantic and syntactic acceptability by children. *Journal of Psycholinguistic Research, 1972, 1,* 299–310.

Denney, D. R. The effects of exemplary and cognitive models and self-rehearsal on children's interpretative strategies. *Journal of Experimental Child Psychology, 1975, 19,* 476–488.

Denney, N. W., & Turner, M. C. Facilitating cognitive performance in children: A comparison of strategy modeling and strategy modeling with overt self-verbalization. *Journal of Experimental Child Psychology, 1979, 28,* 119–131.

Donaldson, M. *Children's minds*. London: Fontana, 1977.

Donaldson, M., & Balfour, G. Less is more: A study of language comprehension in children. *British Journal of Psychology, 1968, 59,* 461–471.

Dore, J. "Oh them Sheriff": A pragmatic analysis of children's responses to questions. In S. Ervin-Tripp & C. Mitchell-Kernan (Eds.), *Child discourse*. New York: Academic Press, 1977.

Dore, J. What's so conceptual about the acquisition of linguistic structures? *Journal of Child Language, 1979, 6(1),* 129–138.

Dougherty, J. W. D. Saliency and relativity in classification. *American Ethnologist, 1978, 5,* 66–80.

Dudycha, G. J., & Dudycha, M. M. Some factors and characteristics of childhood memories. *Child Development, 1933, 4,* 265–278.

Ellis, N. R. Memory processes in retardates and normals. In N. R. Ellis (Ed.), *International review of research in mental retardation* (Vol. 4). New York: Academic Press, 1970.

Ervin-Tripp, S. An overview of grammatical development. In D. Slobin (Ed.), *The ontogenesis of grammar*. New York: Academic Press, 1971.

Ervin-Tripp, S. Is Sybil there? The structure of some American English directives. *Language and Society*, 1976, *5*, 25–26.

Ervin-Tripp, S. Speech acts and social learning. In K. Basso and H. Selby (Eds.), *Meaning in anthropology*. Albuquerque: University of New Mexico Press, 1977.

Ervin-Tripp, S. Whatever happened to communicative competence? In *Proceedings of the linguistic forum*. Champaign-Urbana, Ill.: University of Illinois, 1978.

Ervin-Tripp, S., & Mitchell-Kernan, C. *Child discourse*. New York: Academic Press, 1977.

Fein, D. J. Prevalence of speech and language impairments. *American Speech, Language and Hearing Association*, 1983, *25*(2), 37–39.

Ferreiro, E., & Sinclair, H. Temporal relations in language. *International Journal of Psychology*, 1971, *6*, 39–47.

Fillmore, C. J. The case for case. In E. Bach & R. T. Harms (Eds.), *Universals in linguistic theory*. New York: Holt, Rinehart, & Winston, 1968.

Fillmore, C. The case for case reopened. In P. Cole & J. M. Sadock (Eds.), *Syntax and semantics* (Vol. 8), *Grammatical relations*. New York: Academic Press, 1977.

Fischer, K. W. A theory of cognitive development: The control and construction of hierarchies of skills. *Psychological Review*, 1980, *87*(6), 477–531.

Fischer, K. W., & Corrigan, R. A. A skill approach to language development. In R. Stark (Ed.), *Language behavior in infancy and early childhood*. Amsterdam: Elsevier-North Holland, 1981.

Flavell, J. H. *The developmental psychology of Jean Piaget*. New York: D. Van Nostrand Co., 1963.

Flavell, J. H. Developmental studies of mediated memory. In H. W. Reese & L. P. Lipsitt (Eds.), *Advances in child development and behavior* (Vol. 5). New York: Academic Press, 1970.

Flavell, J. H., Beach, D. R., & Chinsky, J. M. Spontaneous verbal rehearsal in a memory task as a function of age. *Child Development*, 1966, *37*, 283–299.

Fletcher, P. The development of the verb phrase. In P. Fletcher & M. Garman (Eds.), *Language acquisition*. Cambridge, England: Cambridge University Press, 1979.

Flores d'Arcais, G. B. The acquisition of subordinating constructions in children's language. In R. Campbell & P. T. Smith (Eds.), *Recent advances in the psychology of language: Language development and mother-child interaction.* New York: Plenum, 1978.

Fodor, J. A. *The language of thought.* Cambridge, Mass.: Harvard University Press, 1979.

Fodor, J. A., Bever, T. G., & Garrett, M. F. *The psychology of language.* New York: McGraw-Hill, 1974.

Folger, M. K., & Leonard, L. B. Language and sensorimotor development during the early period of referential speech. *Journal of Speech and Hearing Research,* 1978, 21(3), 519–527.

Foss, D.J., & Hakes, D. T. *Psycholinguistics: An introduction to the psychology of language.* Englewood Cliffs, N.J.: Prentice-Hall, 1978.

Foster, S. H. *From non-verbal to verbal communication: A study of the development of topic initiation strategies during the first two-and-a-half years.* Unpublished doctoral dissertation, University of Lancaster, England, 1979.

Fowles, B., & Glanz, M. E. Competence and talent in verbal riddle comprehension. *Journal of Child Language,* 1977, 4, 433–452.

Furth, H. G. *Thinking without language: Psychological implications of deafness.* New York: The Free Press, 1966.

Furth, H. G., & Milgram, N. A. Labeling and grouping effects in the recall of pictures by children. *Child Development,* 1973, 44, 511–518.

Gardner, H., Kircher, M., Winner, E., & Perkins, D. Children's metaphoric productions and preferences. *Journal of Child Language,* 1975, 2, 125–141.

Gardner, H., Winner, E., Bechhofer, R., & Wolf, D. The development of figurative language. In K. Nelson (Ed.), *Children's language* (Vol. 1). New York: Gardner, 1978.

Garvey, C. Requests and responses in children's speech. *Journal of Child Language,* 1975, 2, 41–63.

Garvey, C. *Play.* Cambridge, Mass.: Harvard University Press, 1977.

Gleitman, L. R., Gleitman, H., & Shipley, E. F. The emergence of the child as grammarian. *Cognition,* 1972, 1, 137–164.

Goodluck, H. Children's grammar of complement-subject interpretation. In S. L. Tavakolian (Ed.), *Language acquisition and linguistic theory.* Cambridge, Mass.: MIT Press, 1981.

Goulet, L. R. Verbal learning and memory research with retardates: An attempt to assess developmental trends. In N. R. Ellis (Ed.), *International review of research in mental retardation* (Vol. 3). New York: Academic Press, 1968.

Greenfield, P., Nelson, K., & Saltzman, E. The development of rulebound strategies for manipulating seriated cups: A parallel between action and grammar. *Cognitive Psychology*, 1972, *3*, 291–310.

Greenwald, C. A., & Leonard, L. B. Communicative and sensorimotor development of Down's syndrome children. *American Journal of Mental Deficiency*, 1979, *84*(3), 296–303.

Gruendel, J. Referential extension in early language development. *Child Development*, 1977, *48*(4), 1567–1576.

Gumperz, J. J. Introduction. In J. J. Gumperz & D. Hymes (Eds.), *Directions in sociolinguistics: The ethnography of communication.* New York: Holt, Rinehart, and Winston, 1972.

Gumperz, J. J., & Hymes, D. Ethnography of communication. *American Anthropologist*, 1964, Special Issue No. 6.

Hagen, J., & Kingsley, R. P. Label effects in short-term memory. *Child Development*, 1968, *39*, 113–121.

Hakes, D. T. *The development of metalinguistic abilities in children.* Berlin: Springer-Verlag, 1980.

Hardy-Brown, K., Plomin, R., & DeFries, J. C. Genetic and environmental influences on the rate of communicative development in the first year of life. *Developmental Psychology*, 1981, *17*, 704–717.

Hirsch-Pasek, K., Gleitman, L. R., & Gleitman, H. What does the brain say to the mind? A study of the detection and report of ambiguity by young children. In A. Sinclair, R. J. Jarvella, & W. J. M. Levelt (Eds.), *The child's conception of language.* Berlin: Springer-Verlag, 1978.

Hirst, W., & Weil, J. Acquisition of epistemic and deontic meaning of models. *Journal of Child Language*, 1982, *9*, 659–666.

Howe, H. E., & Hillman, D. The acquisition of semantic restrictions by children. *Journal of Verbal Learning and Verbal Behavior*, 1973, *12*, 132–139.

Hudson, L. M., Guthrie, K. H., & Santilli, N. R. The use of linguistic and non-linguistic strategies in kindergartners' interpretations of 'more' and 'less.' *Journal of Child Language*, 1982, *9*, 125–138.

Hull, C. L. *Principles of behavior.* New York: Appleton-Century-Crofts, 1943.

Huston, A. C. Sex typing. In P. H. Mussen and E. M. Hetherington (Eds.), *Handbook of child psychology* (4th ed.) (Vol. 4), *Socialization, personality and social development.* New York: Wiley, 1983.

Huston-Stein, A., & Wright, J. C. Children and television: Effects of the medium, its content, and its form. *Journal of Research and Development in Education*, 1979, *13*, 20–31.

Huttenlocker, J., & Lui, F. The semantic organization of some simple nouns and verbs. *Journal of Verbal Learning and Verbal Behavior*, 1979, *18*, 141–162.

Hymes, D. The ethnography of speaking. In T. Gladwin & W. C. Sturtevant (Eds.), *Anthropology and human behavior*, Washington, D. C.: American Anthropological Association, 1962, 13–53.

Hymes, D. Formal discussion. In U. Bellugi & R. Brown (eds.), *The acquisition of language. Monographs of the Society for Research in Child Development*, 1964, *29*, Serial No. 92, 107–112.

Hymes, D. Competence and performance in linguistic theory. In R. Huxley & E. Ingram (Eds.), *Language acquisition: Models and methods*. New York: Academic Press, 1971.

Hymes, D. On communicative competence. In J. B. Pride & J. Holmes (eds.), *Sociolinguistics*. Harmondsworth, England: Penguin, 1972.

Ingram, D. If and when transformations are acquired by children. In D. P. Dato (Ed.), *Developmental psycholinguistics: Theory and applications*. Washington, D. C.: Georgetown University Press, 1975.

Inhelder, B. Cognitive development and its contributions to diagnosis of some phenomena of mental deficiency. *Merrill-Palmer Quarterly*, 1966, *12*, 299–317.

Inhelder, B., & Karmiloff-Smith, A. Thought and languge. In B. Z. Presseisen, D. Goldstein, & M. H. Appel (Eds.), *Topics in cognitive development* (Vol. 2). New York: Plenum, 1978.

Inhelder, B., & Piaget, J. *The growth of logical thinking from childhood to adolescence*. New York: Basic Books, 1958.

Inhelder, B., & Piaget, J. *The early growth of logical thinking*. New York: Norton, 1964.

Jarvis, P. E. Verbal control of sensori-motor performance. A test of Luria's hypotheses. *Human Development*, 1968, *11*, 171–183.

James, S. L., & Miller, J. F. Children's awareness of semantic constraints in sentences. *Child Development*, 1973, *44*, 69–76.

Jenson, A. R., & Frederiksen, J. Free recall of categorizable and uncategorizable lists: A test of the Jensen hypothesis. *Journal of Educational Psychology*, 1973, *3*, 304–314.

Johnston, J. R. *A study of spatial thought and expression: In back and in front*. Unpublished doctoral dissertation, University of California at Berkeley, 1979.

Johnston, J. R. The language disordered child. In N. Lass, J. Northern, D. Yoder, & L. McReynolds (Eds.), *Speech, language and hearing*. Philadelphia: W. B. Saunders Co., 1982. (a)

Johnston, J. R. Narratives: A new look at communication problems in older language-disordered children. *Language, Speech and Hearing Services in the Schools*, 1982, *13*(3), 144–155. (b)

Johnston, J. R. Interpreting the Leiter IQ: Performance profiles of young normal and language-disordered children. *Journal of Speech and Hearing Research,* in press.

Johnston, J. R., & Ramsted, V. Cognitive development in preadolescent language impaired children. *British Journal of Disorders of Communication,* 1983, *18,* 49–55.

Johnston, J. R., & Schery, T. The use of grammatical morphemes by children with communication disorders. In D. Morehead & A. Morehead (Eds.), *Normal and deficient child language.* Baltimore: University Park Press, 1976.

Johnston, J. R., & Slobin, D. I. The development of locative expressions in English, Italian, Serbo-Croatian and Turkish. *Journal of Child Language,* 1979, *6*(13), 529–545.

Johnston, J. R., & Weismer, S. E. Mental rotation abilities in language disordered children. *Journal of Speech and Hearing Research,* 1983, *26,* 397–403.

Joynt, D., & Cambourne, D. Psycholinguistic development and the control of behavior. *British Journal of Educational Psychology,* 1968, *38,* 249–260.

Kagen, J., Interviewed by Elizabeth Hall. The fearful child's hidden talents. *Psychology Today,* 1982, *16*(7), 50–59.

Kail, R. C. Children's encoding of taxonomic classes and subclasses. *Developmental Psychology,* 1976, *12,* 487–488.

Kamhi, A. G. Nonlinguistic symbolic and conceptual abilities of language impaired and normally developing children. *Journal of Speech and Hearing Research,* 1981, *24,* 446–453.

Kamhi, A. G., & Johnston, J. R. Towards an understanding of retarded children's linguistic deficiencies. *Journal of Speech and Hearing Research,* 1982, *25*(3), 435–445.

Kaplan, R. M., & Bresnan, J. Lexical functional grammars: A formal system for grammatical representation. In J. Bresnan (Ed.), *The mental representation of grammatical relations.* Cambridge, Mass.: MIT Press, 1982.

Karmiloff-Smith, A. The interplay between syntax, semantics and phonology in language acquisition processes. In R. N. Campbell & P. T. Smith (Eds.), *Recent advances in the psychology of language: Language development and mother-child interaction.* New York: Plenum, 1978.

Karmiloff-Smith, A. *A functional approach to child language.* Cambridge, England: Cambridge University Press, 1979.

Kay, D., & Anglin, J. Overextension and underextension in the child's expressive and receptive speech. *Journal of Child Language,* 1982, *9*(1), 83–98.

Keenen, E. O. Conversational competence in children. *Journal of Child Language,* 1974, *1,* 163–183.

Keil, F. C. *Semantic and conceptual development.* Cambridge, Mass.: Harvard University Press, 1979.

Kellas, G., Ashcraft, M., & Johnson, N. Rehearsal processes in the short-term memory performance of mildly retarded adolescents. *American Journal of Mental Deficiency,* 1973, *73,* 670–679.

Kemper, S. The development of narrative skills: Explanations and entertainments. In S. A. Kuczaj (Ed.) *Discourse development.* Hillsdale, N. J.: Erlbaum Associates, 1984.

Kendler, T. S. An ontogeny of mediational deficiency. *Child Development,* 1972, *43,* 1–17.

Kendler, T. S. The development of learning: A levels of functioning explanation. In H. W. Reese & L. P. Lipsitt (Eds.), *Advances in child development and behavior* (Vol. 13). New York: Academic Press, 1979.

Kendler, T. S., & Kendler, H. H. Reversal and nonreversal shifts in kindergarten children. *Journal of Experimental Psychology,* 1959, *58,* 56–60.

Kenney, T. J., Cannizzo, S. R., & Flavell, J. H. Spontaneous vs. induced verbal rehearsal in a recall task. *Child Development,* 1967, *38,* 953–966.

Kessler, C. V. Post semantic processes in delayed child language related to first and second language learning. In D. P. Dato (Ed.), *Development of psycholinguistics: Theory and applications.* Washington, D. C.: Georgetown University, 1975.

Kingsley, D. R., & Hagen, J. W. Induced versus spontaneous rehearsal in short term memory in nursery school children. *Developmental Psychology,* 1969, *1,* 40–46.

Kintsch, W. Models of free recall and recognition. In D. A. Norman (Ed.), *Models of human memory.* New York: Academic Press, 1970.

Kobasigawa, A. Utilization of retrieval cues by children in recall. *Child Development,* 1974, *45,* 127–134.

Kobasigawa, A., & Middleton, D. B. Free recall of categorized Femsby children at three grade levels. *Child Development,* 1972, *43,* 1067–1072.

Kohlberg, L., Yaeger, J., & Hjertholm, E. Private speech: Four studies and a review of theories. *Child Development,* 1968, *39,* 691–736.

Kosslyn, S. R. *Image and mind.* Cambridge, Mass.: Harvard University Press, 1980.

Kuczaj, S. A. Why do children fail to overgeneralize the progressive inflection? *Journal of Child Language,* 1978, *5,* 167–171.

Kuczaj, S. A. The acquisition of word meaning in the context of the development of the semantic system. In C. Brainerd and M. Pressley (Eds.), *Progress in cognitive development research,*

(Vol. 2), *Verbal processes in children*. New York: Springer-Verlag, 1982, 95–124. (a)

Kuczaj, S. A. On the nature of syntactic development. In S. A. Kuczaj (Ed.), *Language development* (Vol. 1). Hillsdale, N. J.: Erlbaum Associates, 1982. (b)

Kuczaj, S. A., & Maratsos, M. P. On the acquisition of front, back, and side. *Child Development*, 1975, *46*, 202–210.

Kuenne, M. R. Experimental investigation of the relation of language to transposition behavior in young children. *Journal of Experimental Psychology*, 1946, *36*, 471–490.

Kusché, C. A., & Greenberg, M. T. Evaluative understanding and role-taking ability: A comparison of deaf and hearing children. *Child Development*, 1983, *54*, 141–147.

Labov, W. *Sociolinguistic patterns*. Philadelphia: University of Pennsylvania Press, 1972.

Lange, G. The development of conceptual and rote recall skills among school age children. *Journal of Experimental Child Psychology*, 1973, *15*, 394–406.

Lange, G. Organizational-related processes in children's recall. In P. A. Ornstein (Ed.), *Memory development in children*. Hillsdale, N. J.: Erlbaum Associates, 1978.

Lenneberg, E. H. A probablistic approach to language learning. *Behavioral Science*, 1957, *2*, 1–12.

Lenneberg, E. H. *Biological foundations of language*. New York: Wiley, 1967.

Leonard, L. B. What is deviant language? *Journal of Speech and Hearing Disorders*, 1972, *37*, 427–446.

Leonard, L. B. Language impairment in children. *Merrill-Palmer Quarterly*, 1979, *25*(3), 205–232.

Leonard, L. B., & Schwartz, R. Early linguistic development of children with specific language impairment. In K. E. Nelson (Ed.), *Children's language* (Vol. 6). New York: Gardner Press, in press.

Levine, S. C., & Carey, S. Up front: The acquisition of a concept and a word. *Journal of Child Language*, 1982, *9*(3), 645–658.

Liberman, A. M. On finding that speech is special. *American Psychologist*, 1982, *37*(2), 148–167.

Limber, J. The genesis of complex sentences. In T. E. Moore (Ed.), *Cognitive development and the acquisition of language*. New York: Academic Press, 1973.

Linton, M. Memory for real-world events. In D. A. Normal and D. E. Rumelhart (Eds.), *Explorations in cognition*. San Francisco: Freeman, 1975.

Linton, M. Transformations of memory in everyday life. In U.

Neisser (Ed.), *Memory observed: Remembering in natural contexts.* San Francisco: Freeman, 1982.

Lubert, N. Auditory perceptual impairments in children with specific language disorders: A review of the literature. *Journal of Speech and Hearing Disorders,* 1981, *46*(1), 3–9.

Luria, A. R. *The role of speech in the regulation of normal and abnormal behavior.* New York: Liveright, 1961.

Luria, A. R. *Cognitive development: Its cultural and social foundations.* Cambridge, Mass.: Harvard University Press, 1976.

Macnamara, J. Cognitive basis of language learning in infants. *Psychological Review,* 1972, *79*(1), 1–13.

Macnamara, J. Children's command of the logic of conversation. In J. Macnamara (Ed.), *Language learning and thought.* New York: Academic Press, 1977, 261–288.

Macnamara, J. *Names for things: A study of human learning.* Cambridge, Mass.: MIT Press, 1982.

Macnamara, J., Baker, E., & Olson, C. L. Four-year-olds' understanding of *pretend, forget,* and *know:* Evidence for propositional operations. *Child Development,* 1976, *47,* 62–70.

MacWhinney, B. Rules, rote, and analogy in morphological formation by Hungarian children. *Journal of Child Language,* 1975, *10,* 153–165.

MacWhinney, B. The acquisition of morphophonology. *Monographs of the Society for Research in Child Development,* 1978, Serial No. 174.

MacWhinney, B. Basic syntactic processes. In S. A. Kuczaj (Ed.), *Language development* (Vol. 1). Hillsdale, N. J.: Lawrence Erlbaum Associates, 1982.

Mandler, G. Organization and memory. In K. W. Spence & J. T. Spence (Eds.), *The psychology of learning and motivation* (Vol. 2). New York: Academic Press, 1968.

Mandler, J. M. A code in the node: The use of story schema in retrieval. *Discourse Processes,* 1978, *1,* 14–35.

Mandler, J. M. Categorical and schematic organization in memory. In C. R. Puff (Ed.), *Memory, organization and struction.* New York: Academic Press, 1979.

Mandler, J. M. Representation. In J. H. Flavell & E. M. Markman (Eds.), *Cognitive development,* (Vol. 3) of P. Mussen (Ed.), *Manual of child psychology.* New York: Wiley, 1983.

Maratsos, M. P. *The use of definite and indefinite reference in young children.* Cambridge, England: Cambridge University Press, 1976.

Maratsos, M. P. New models in linguistic and language acquisition. In M. Halle, J. Bresnan, & G. A. Miller (eds.), *Linguistic* *theory and psychological reality.* Cambridge, Mass.: MIT Press, 1978.

Maratsos, M. P. How to get from words to sentences. In D. Aaronson and R. J. Rieber (Eds.), *Psycholinguistic research: Implications and applications.* Hillsdale, N. J.: Lawrence Erlbaum Associates, 1979. (a)

Maratsos, M. P. Learning how and when to use pronouns and determiners. In P. Fletcher & M. Garman (Eds.), *Language acquisition.* Cambridge, England: Cambridge University Press, 1979. (b)

Maratsos, M. P., & Chalkley, M. A. The internal language of children's syntax: The ontogenesis and representation of syntactic categories. In K. Nelson (Ed.), *Children's language* (Vol. 2). New York: Gardner, 1980.

Maratsos, M. P., & Kuczaj, S. A. Preschool children's use of NOT and N'T: NOT is not (ISN'T N'T). *Papers and Reports in Child Language* (Stanford University), 1976, *12,* 157–168.

Maratsos, M. P., & Kuczaj, S. A. Against the transformationalist account: A simpler analysis of auxiliary overmarkings. *Journal of Child Language,* 1978, *5,* 337–345.

Maratsos, M. P., Kuczaj, S. A., Fox, D. E. C., & Chalkley, M. A. Some empirical studies in the acquisition of transformational relations: Passives, negatives, and the past tense. In W. A. Collins (Ed.), *Children's language and communication.* Hillsdale, N. J.: Lawrence Erlbaum Associates, 1979.

Masur, E. F. Mothers' responses to infants' object-related gestures: Influences on lexical development. *Journal of Child Language,* 1982, *9*(1), 23–30.

McCawley, J. D. Prelexical syntax. In R. J. O'Brien (Ed.), *Monograph series on language and linguistics.* Washington, D. C.: Georgetown University Press, 1971.

McCune-Nicolich, L. The cognitive bases of relational words in the single word period. *Journal of Child Language,* 1981, *8*(1), 15–34. (a)

McCune-Nicolich, L. Toward symbolic functioning: Structure of early pretend games and potential parallels with language. *Child Development,* 1981, *52*(3), 785–797. (b)

McGhee, P. E. Cognitive mastery and children's humor. *Psychological Bulletin,* 1974, *81,* 721–730.

Meacham, J. A. Verbal guidance through remembering the goals of actions. *Child Development,* 1978, *49,* 188–194.

Meadow, K. P. The development of deaf children. In M. Hetherington (Ed.), *Review of child development research,* (Vol. 5). Chicago: University of Chicago Press, 1975.

Meichenbaum, D., & Goodman, J. The development of control of operant motor responding by verbal operants. *Journal of Experimental Child Psychology,* 1969, *7,* 553–565.

Menyuk, P. Comparison of grammar of children with functionally deviant and normal speech. *Journal of Speech and Hearing Research,* 1964, *7,* 109–121.

Mervis, C. B., & Rosch, E. Categorization of natural objects. *Annual Review of Psychology,* 1981, *32,* 89–115.

Miller, J. F. Early psycholinguistic acquisition. In R. L. Schiefelbusch and D. D. Bricker (Eds.), *Early language: Acquisition and intervention.* Baltimore: University Park Press, 1981.

Miller, J. F., Chapman, R. S., Branston, M. B., & Reichle, J. Language comprehension in sensorimotor stages V and VI. *Journal of Speech and Hearing Research,* 1980, *23*(2), 284–311.

Miller, J. F., & Yoder, D. An ontogenetic language teaching strategy for retarded children. In R. L. Schiefelbusch and L. Lloyd (Eds.), *Language perspectives: Acquisition, retardation, and intervention.* Baltimore: University Park Press, 1974.

Miller, S. R., Shelton, J., & Flavell, J. H. A test of Luria's hypothesis concerning the development of self-regulation. *Child Development,* 1970, *41,* 651–665.

Moely, B. E., Olson, F. A., Halwes, T. G., & Flavell, J. H. Production deficiency in young children's clustered recall. *Developmental Psychology,* 1969, *1,* 26–34.

Moores, D. *Educating the deaf: Psychology, principles, and practices.* Boston: Houghton Mifflin Co., 1978.

Morehead, D. M., & Ingram, D. The development of base syntax in normal and linguistically deviant children. *Journal of Speech and Hearing Research,* 1973, *16,* 330–352.

Morehead, D. M., & Ingram, D. The development of base syntax in normal and linguistically deviant children. In D. M. Morehead & A. E. Morehead (Eds.), *Normal and deficient child language.* Baltimore: University Park Press, 1976.

Morehead, D. M., & Morehead, A. From signal to sign: A Piagetian view of thought and language during the first two years. In R. L. Schiefelbusch and L. L. Lloyd (eds.), *Language perspectives: Acquisition, retardation and intervention.* Baltimore: University Park Press, 1974.

Myers, N. A., & Perlmutter, M. Memory in the years from two to five. In P. A. Ornstein (Ed.), *Memory development in children.* Hillsdale, N. J.: Lawrence Erlbaum Associates, 1978.

Neimark, E. D. Natural language concepts: Additional evidence. *Child Development,* 1974, *45,* 508–511.

Neimark, E. D., Slotnick, N. S., & Ulrich, T. Development of memorization strategies. *Developmental Psychology,* 1971, *5,* 427–432.

Nelson, K. Structure and strategy in learning to talk. *Monographs of the Society for Research in Child Development,* 1973, *149,* Serial No. 38, 1–2.

Nelson, K. Concept, word and sentence: Interrelations in acquisition and development. *Psychological Review,* 1974, *81,* 267–285. (a)

Nelson, K. Variations in children's concepts by age and category. *Child Development,* 1974, *45,* 577–584. (b)

Nelson, K. Social cognition in a script framework. In L. Ross & J. Flavell (eds.), *The development of social cognition in childhood.* New York: Cambridge University Press, 1981.

Nelson, K., & Gruendel, J. M. At morning it's lunchtime: A scriptal view of children's stories. *Discourse Processes,* 1979, *2,* 73–94.

Newmeyer, F. J. *Linguistic theory in America: The First quarter century of transformational generative grammar.* New York: Academic Press, 1980.

Nye, W. C., McMannis, D. L., & Haugen, D. M. Training and transfer of categorization by retarded adults. *American Journal of Mental Deficiency,* 1972, *77,* 199–207.

Ornstein, P. A., & Naus, M. J. Rehearsal processes in children's memory. In P. A. Ornstein (Ed.), *Memory development in children.* Hillsdale, N. J.: Lawrence Erlbaum Associates, 1978.

Ottem, E. An analysis of cognitive studies with deaf subjects. *American Annals of the Deaf,* 1980, *125,* 564–575.

Paivio, A., & Begg, I. *The psychology of language.* Englewood Cliffs, N.J.: Prentice-Hall, 1981.

Palmer, F. R. *Semantics: A new outline.* Cambridge, England: Cambridge University Press, 1976.

Paris, S. G. *Propositional and logical thinking and comprehension of logical connectives: A developmental analysis.* The Hague: Mouton, 1975.

Pea, R. D. Origins of verbal logic: Spontaneous denials by two- and three-year olds. *Journal of Child Language,* 1982, *9,* 597–626.

Perlmutter, M., & Meyers, N. A. Development of recall in 2- to 4-year old children. *Developmental Psychology,* 1979, *15,* 73–83.

Piaget, J. *The language and thought of the child.* New York: Meridian Books, 1955.

Piaget, J. *Play, dreams, and imitation in childhood.* New York: Norton, 1962.

Piaget, J. Piaget's theory. In P. H. Mussen (Ed.), *Carmichael's manual of child psychology* (3rd ed.). New York: John Wiley, 1970.

Piaget, J., & Inhelder, B. *The psychology of the child.* New York: Basic Books, 1969.

Piatelli-Palmarini, M. *Language and learning: The debate between Jean Piaget and Noam Chomsky.* Cambridge, Mass.: Harvard University Press, 1980.

Pinker, S. Formal models of language learning. *Cognition,* 1979, *7,* 217–283.

Pinker, S. A theory of the acquisition of lexical interpretative grammars. In J. Bresnan (Ed.), *The mental representation of grammatical relation.* Cambridge, Mass.: MIT Press, 1982.

Quay, L. C., Hough, R. A., Mathews, M., & Jarrett, O. S. Predictors of communication encoding: Age, SES, and cognitive ability. *Developmental Psychology,* 1981, *17*(2), 221–223.

Quigley, S. P., & Kretschmer, R. E. *The education of deaf children: Issues, theory, and practice.* Baltimore: University Park Press, 1982.

Read, B., & Cherry, L. J. Preschool children's production of directive forms. *Discourse Processes,* 1978, *1,* 233–245.

Rees, N. S. Auditory processing factors in language disorders: The view from Procrustes' bed. *Journal of Speech and Hearing Disorders,* 1973, *38,* 304–315.

Reese, H. W. Verbal mediation as a function of age level. *Psychological Bulletin,* 1962, *59,* 502–506.

Rice, M. L. Identification of children with language disorders. In R. L. Schiefelbusch (Ed.), *Language intervention strategies.* Baltimore: University Park Press, 1978.

Rice, M. L. *Cognition to language: Categories, word meanings and training.* Baltimore: University Park Press, 1980.

Rice, M. L. Contemporary accounts of the cognition/language relationship: Implications for language clinicians. *Journal of Speech and Hearing Disorders,* 1983, *48*(4), 347–359.

Rice, M. L. A cognition account of differences between children's comprehension and production of language. *Western Journal of Speech Communication,* 1984, *48,* 145–154. (a)

Rice, M. L. Cognitive aspects of communicative development. In R. L. Schiefelbusch and J. Pickar (Eds.), *The acquisition of communicative competence.* Baltimore: University Park Press, 1984. (b)

Rieber, R. W., & Vetter, H. Theoretical and historical roots of psycholinguistic research. In R. W. Rieber (Ed.), *Psychology of language and thought.* New York: Plenum, 1980.

Rosch, E. On the internal structure of perceptual and semantic categories. In T. E. Moore (Ed.), *Cognitive development and the acquisition of language.* New York: Academic Press, 1973.

Rosch, E., & Mervis, C. B. Family resemblances: Studies in the internal structure of categories. *Cognitive Psychology,* 1975, *7*(4), 573–605.

Rosch, E., Mervis, C. B., Gray, W. D., Johnson, P. M., & Boyes-Braem, P. Basic objects in natural categories. *Cognitive Psychology*, 1976, *8*, 382–439.

Rosch, R. Human categorization. In N. Warren (Ed.), *Studies in cross-cultural psychology*. London: Academic, 1977.

Rosner, S. R., & Hayes, D. S. A developmental study of category item production. *Child Development*, 1977, *48*, 1062–1065.

Ross, D. M., Ross, S. A., & Downing, M. L. Intentional training vs. observational learning of mediation strategies in EMR children. *American Journal of Mental Deficiency*, 1973, *78*, 292–299.

Rossi, S., & Wittrock, M. C. Developmental shifts in verbal recall between mental ages two and five. *Child Development*, 1971, *42*, 333–338.

Sachs, J. S., Bard, B., & Johnson, M. L. Language learning with restricted input: Case studies of two hearing children of deaf parents. *Applied Psycholinguistics (Journal of Child Language)*, 1981, *2*(1), 33–54.

Sachs, J. S., & Johnson, M. Language development in a hearing child of deaf parents. In W. von Raffler Engel and Y. LeBrun (Eds.), *Baby talk and infant speech* (Neurolingusitics 5). Amsterdam: Swets and Zeitlinger, 1976.

Salatas, H., & Flavell, J. H. Retrieval of recently learned information: Development of strategies and control skills. *Child Development*, 1976, *47*, 941–948.

Schachtel, E. G. *Metamorphosis*. New York: Basic Books, 1959.

Schaff, A. *Language and cognition*. (R. S. Cohen, Ed.). New York: McGraw-Hill, 1973.

Schank, R. C., & Abelson, R. *Scripts, plans, goals and understanding*. Hillsdale, N. J.: Lawrence Erlbaum Associates, 1977.

Schegloff, E. A. Sequencing in conversational openings. *American Anthropologist*, 1968, *70*, 1075–1095.

Schlesinger, I. M. The production of utterances and language acquisition. In D. I. Slobin (Ed.), *The ontogenesis of grammar*. New York: Academic Press, 1971.

Schlesinger, I. M. The role of cognitive development and linguistic input in language acquisition. *Journal of Child Language*, 1977, *4*, 153–169.

Schlesinger, I. M. *Steps to language: Toward a theory of native language acquisition*. Hillsdale, N. J.: Lawrence Erlbaum Associates, 1982.

Scholl, D. M., & Ryan, E. B. Child judgments of sentences varying in grammatical complexity. *Journal of Experimental Child Psychology*, 1975, *20*, 274–285.

Scribner, S., & Cole, M. Effects of constrained recall training on children's performance in a verbal memory task. *Child Development*, 1972, *43*, 845–857.

Sheingold, K., & Tenney, Y. J. Memory for a salient childhood event. In U. Neisser (Ed.), *Memory observed: Remembering in natural contexts*. San Francisco: Freeman, 1982.

Shields, M. M. The child as psychologist: Construing the social world. In A. Lock (Ed.), *Action, gesture and symbol: The emergence of language*. London: Academic Press, 1978.

Shiffrin, R. M. Memory search. In D. A. Norman (Ed.), *Models of memory*. New York: Academic Press, 1970.

Shultz, T. R. A cognitive developmental analysis of humor. In A. J. Chapman & H. C. Foole (Eds.), *Humor and laughter: Theory, research and applications*. London: John Wiley, 1976.

Shultz, T. R., & Horibe, F. Development of the appreciation of verbal jokes. *Developmental Psychology*, 1974, *10*, 13–20.

Siegel, L. S. Infant tests as predictors of cognitive and language development at two years. *Child Development*, 1981, *52*(2), 545–557.

Siegel, L. S., Lees, A., Allan, L., & Bolton, B. Non-verbal assessment of Piagetian concepts in preschool children with language disabilities. *Educational Psychology*, 1981, *1*, 153–158.

Sinclair, H. J. Sensorimotor action patterns as a condition for the acquisition of syntax. In R. Huxley & D. Ingram (Eds.), *Language acquisition: Models and methods*. New York, Academic Press, 1971.

Sinclair, H. J. The relevance of Piaget's early work for a semantic approach to language acquisition. In B. Z. Presseisen, D. Goldstein, & M. A. Appel (Eds.), *Topics in cognitive development* (Vol. 2). New York: Plenum, 1978.

Sinclair, H. J., & Ferreiro, E. Temporal relationships in language. *International Journal of Psychology*, 1971, *6*, 39–47.

Sinclair–de Zwart, H. Developmental psycholinguistics. In D. Elkind & J. H. Flavell (Eds.), *Studies in cognitive development*. New York: Oxford University Press, 1969.

Sinclair–de Zwart, H. Language acquisition and cognitive development. In T. E. Moore (Ed.), *Cognitive development and the acquisition of language*. New York: Academic Press, 1973.

Slobin, D. I. Soviet psycholinguistics. In N. O'Connor (Ed.), *Present day Russian psychology: A symposium by seven authors*. Oxford, England: Pergammon Press, 1966.

Slobin, D. I. (Ed.). *A field manual for cross-cultural study of the acquisition of communicative competence*. Berkeley: A. S. U. C. Bookstore, 1967.

Slobin, D. I. Cognitive prerequisite for the development of grammar. In C. A. Ferguson & D. I. Slobin (Eds.), *Studies of child language development*. New York: Holt, Rinehart, and Winston, 1973, 175–208.

Slobin, D. I. Language change in childhood and history. In J. Macnamara (Ed.), *Language, learning and thought*. New York: Academic Press, 1977.

Slobin, D. I. *Psycholinguistics* (2nd ed). Glenview, Ill.: Scott, Foresman, 1979.

Slobin, D. I. Universal and particular in the acquisition of language. In L. Gleitman & E. Wanner (Eds.), *Language acquisition: State of the art*. New York: Cambridge University Press, 1982.

Smolak, L. Cognitive precursors of receptive vs. expressive language. *Journal of Child Language*, 1982, 9(1), 13–22.

Snow, C. E., Arlman-Rupp, A., Hassing, Y., Jobse, J., Joosten, J., & Vorster, J. Mothers' speech in three social classes. *Journal of Psycholinguistic Research*, 1976, 5, 1–20.

Snyder, L. Communicative and cognitive abilities and disabilities in the sensorimotor period. *Merrill-Palmer Quarterly*, 1978, 24, 161–180.

Solan, L. The acquisition of structural restrictions on anaphora. In S. L. Tavakolian (Ed.), *Language acquisition and linguistic theory*. Cambridge, Mass.: MIT Press, 1981.

Staats, A. *Learning, language, and cognition*. New York: Holt, Rinehart, & Winston, 1968.

Steckol, K. F., & Leonard, L. B. Sensorimotor development and the use of prelinguistic performatives. *Journal of Speech and Hearing Research*, 1981, 24(2), 262–268.

Steinberg, D. D. *Psycholinguistics: Language, mind and world*. London: Longman, 1982.

Strohner, H., & Nelson, K. E. The young child's development of sentence comprehension: Influence of event probability, nonverbal context, syntactic form, and strategies. *Child Development*, 1974, 45, 567–576.

Stross, B. Acquisition of botanical terminology by Tzeltal children. In M. Edmonson (Ed.), *Meaning in Mayan languages*. The Hague: Mouton, 1973.

Sudnow, D. (Ed.). *Studies in social interaction*. New York: Free Press, 1972.

Sugarman, S. *A description of communicative development in the prelanguage child*. In I. Markova (Ed.), *The social context of language*. London: Wiley, 1978.

Tager-Flusberg, H. Sentence comprehension in autistic children. *Applied Psycholinguistics*, 1981, 2, 5–24.

Tallal, P., Stark, R., Kallman, C., & Mellits, S. A reexamination of some nonverbal perceptual abilities of language-impaired and normal children as a function of age and sensory modality. *Journal of Speech and Hearing Research,* 1981, *24,* 351–356.

Tavakolian, S. L. The conjoined-clause analysis of relative clauses. In S. L. Tavakolian (Ed.), *Language acquisition and linguistic theory.* Cambridge, Mass.: MIT Press, 1981.

Tighe, T. J., & Tighe, L. S. Reversals prior to solution of concept identification in children. *Journal of Experimental Child Psychology,* 1972, *13,* 488–501.

Tinsley, V. S., & Waters, H. S. The development of verbal control over motor behavior: A replication and extension of Luria's findings. *Child Development,* 1982, *53,* 746–753.

Tremaine, R. V. *Syntax and Piagetian operational thought.* Washington, D. C.: Georgetown University Press, 1975.

Trevarthen, C., & Hubley, P. Secondary intersubjectivity: Confidence confiding, and acts of meaning in the first year. In A. Lock (Ed.), *Action, gesture and symbol.* New York: Academic Press, 1978.

Turner, E. A., & Rommetveit, R. The acquisition of sentence voice and reversibility. *Child Development,* 1967, *38,* 649–660.

Urwin, C. The contribution of nonvisual communication systems and language to knowing oneself. In M. Beveridge (Ed.), *Children thinking through language.* Baltimore: Edward Arnold, 1982.

Uzgiris, I., & Hunt, J. McV. *Assessment in infancy: Ordinal scales of psychological development.* Champaign-Urbana, Ill.: University of Illinois Press, 1975.

Uzgiris, I. C. Experience in the social context: Imitation and play. In R. L. Schiefelbusch and D. Bricker (Eds.), *Early language: Acquisition and intervention.* Baltimore: University Park Press, 1981.

Vaughan, M. E. Clustering, age, and incidental learning. *Journal of Experimental Child Psychology,* 1968, *6,* 323–334.

Veneziano, E. Early language and nonverbal representation: A reassessment. *Journal of Child Language,* 1981, *8,* 541–563.

Vygotsky, L. S. *Thought and language.* Cambridge, Mass.: MIT Press, 1962.

Vygotsky, L. S. *Mind in society: The development of higher psychological processes* (M. Cole, V. John-Steiner, S. Scribner, & E. Souberman, Eds.). Cambridge, Mass: Harvard University Press, 1978.

Waldvogel, S. Childhood memories. Reprinted in U. Neisser (Ed.), *Memory observed: Remembering in natural contexts.* San Francisco: Freeman, 1982.

Wason, P. C., & Johnson-Laird, P. N. *The psychology of reasoning.* Cambridge, Mass.: Harvard University Press, 1972.

Watson-Gegeo, K. A., & Boggs, S. T. From verbal play to talk story: The role of routines in speech events among Hawaiian children. In S. Ervin-Tripp and C. Mitchell-Kernan (Eds.), *Child Discourse.* New York: Academic Press, 1977.

Webb, P. A., & Abrahamson, A. A. Stages of egocentrism in children's use of "this" and "that": A different point of view. *Journal of Child Language,* 1976, *3,* 349–367.

Weil, J., & Stenning, K. A comparison of young children's comprehension and memory for statements of temporal relations. In R. Campbell & P. T. Smith (Eds.), *Recent advances in the psychology of language.* New York: Plenum, 1978.

Wertsch, J. V. From social interaction to higher psychological processes: A clarification and application of Vygotsky's theory. *Human Development,* 1979, *22,* 1–22.

Wertsch, J. V. The role of semiosis in L. S. Vygotsky's theory of human cognition. In B. Bain (Ed.), *The sociogenesis of language and human conduct.* New York: Plenum, 1983.

Wertsch, J. V., Minick, N., & Arns, F. J. The creation of context in joint problem solving action: A cross cultural study. In J. Lave & B. Rogoff (Eds.), *The social context of the development of everyday skills.* Cambridge, Mass.: Harvard University Press, in press.

Wexler, K., & Culicover, P. *Formal principles of language acquisition.* Cambridge, Mass.: MIT Press, 1980.

Whitehurst, G. J. Meaning and semantics. In G. J. Whitehurst & B. J. Zimmerman (Eds.), *The functions of language and cognition.* New York: Academic, 1979.

Whorf, B. *Language, thought, and recall.* Cambridge, Mass.: MIT Press, 1956.

Wiig, E. H., Semel, E. M., & Nystrom, L. A. Comparison of rapid naming abilities in language learning disabled and academically achieving 8-year-olds. *Language, Speech, and Hearing Services in Schools,* 1982, *13*(1), 11–23.

Wilkinson, L. C., Calculator, S., & Dollaghan, C. Ya wanna trade—just for a while: Children's requests and responses to peers. *Discourse Processes,* 1982, *5,* 161–176.

Wimmer, H. Processing of script deviations by young children. *Discourse Processes,* 1979, *2,* 301–310.

Wozniak, R. H. Verbal regulation of motor behavior: Soviet research and non-Soviet replications. *Human Development,* 1972, *15,* 13–57.

Zeamon, D., & House, B. J. The role of attention in retardate discrimination learning. In N. R. Ellis (Ed.), *Handbook of mental deficiency*. New York: McGraw-Hill, 1963.

Zimmerman, B. J., & Whitehurst, G. J. Structure and function: A comparison of two views of the development of language and cognition. In G. J. Whitehurst & B. J. Zimmerman (Eds.), *The functions of language and cognition*. New York: Academic Press, 1979.

Reference Notes

1. Johnston, J. R. *Cognitive prerequisites: The evidence from children learning English*. Paper prepared for the Conference on Cross-linguistic Studies of Language Acquisition, University of California, Berkeley, 1980.
2. Ingram, D. *Stages in the development of one-word utterances*. Paper presented at the Sixth Annual Stanford Child Language Research Forum, Stanford University, April 1974.
3. Eisenburg, A. R. *The acquisition of markers of current relevance*. Paper presented at the Thirteenth Annual Stanford Child Language Research Forum, Stanford University, April 1981.
4. Foster, S. H. *The emergence of topic type in children under 2; 6: A chicken and egg problem*. Paper presented at the Thirteenth Annual Stanford Child Language Research Forum, Stanford University, April 1981.
5. Bowerman, M. *The structure and origin of semantic categories in the language learning child*. Paper prepared for Burg Wartenstein Symposium #74, *Fundamentals of symbolism*, Wenner-Gren Foundation for Anthropological Research, New York, July 16–24, 1977.
6. Roberts, R., & Corbitt, P. Using the theory to predict the development of classification skills. In K. Fischer (Chair), *Sequence and synchrony in cognitive development*. Symposium presented at the American Psychological Association Convention, San Francisco, 1977.
7. Curtiss, S., Kempler, D., & Yamada, J. *Language and cognition in development*. Paper presented at the Biennial Meeting of the Society for Research in Child Development, Boston, April 1981.
8. Curtiss, S., Yamada, J., & Fromkin, V. *How independent is language? On the question of formal parallels between grammar and action*. UCLA Working Papers in Cognitive Linguistics (Vol. 1), Summer, 1979.
9. Fromkin, V. A. *Language and the neurosciences*. UCLA Working Papers in Cognitive Linguistics (Vol. 1), Summer 1979.
10. Hardy-Brown, K. *Genetic and environmental influences on infant communicative development: A study of 50 adopted and 50 nonadopted one-year-old infants*. Paper presented at the 12th Annual Meeting of the Behavior Genetics Association, June 23, 1982.

11. Johnston, J. R., & Kamhi, A. *The same equals less: Syntactic and semantic aspects of the language of language disordered children.* Paper presented at the Symposium on Research in Child Language Disorders, University of Wisconsin, Madison, June 1980.

12. Nelson, K., Fivush, R., Hudson, J., & Lucariello, J. *Scripts and the development of memory.* Paper presented at the Biennial Meeting of the Society for Research in Child Development, Boston, 1981.

13. Abelson, R. P. *The interaction of feelings and goals.* Paper presented at the Social Science Research Council Workshop on the Representation of Cultural Knowledge, San Diego, August 12, 1979.

14. Schank, R. C. *Language and memory.* Paper presented at the La Jolla Conference on Cognitive Science, August 15, 1979.

15. Sack, H. G., & Beilin, H. *Meaning equivalence of active-passive and subject-object first cleft sentences.* Paper presented at the Developmental Psycholinguistics Conference, State University of New York, Buffalo, 1971.

16. Arlin, P. K. *The function of Piagetian operational levels in the preference and production of metaphors.* Paper presented at the Biennial Meeting of the Society for Research in Child Development, April 1977.

17. Stone, C. A., & Wertsch, J. V. *A social interaction analysis of learning disabilities remediation.* Paper presented at the International Conference of the Association for Children with Learning Disabilities, San Francisco, March 1979.

Index